Sensor Projects with Raspberry Pi

Internet of Things and Digital Image Processing

Guillermo Guillen

Apress®

Sensor Projects with Raspberry Pi: Internet of Things and Digital Image Processing

Guillermo Guillen
Ciudad de Mexico, Mexico

ISBN-13 (pbk): 978-1-4842-5298-7   ISBN-13 (electronic): 978-1-4842-5299-4
https://doi.org/10.1007/978-1-4842-5299-4

Managing Director, Apress Media LLC: Welmoed Spahr
Acquisitions Editor: Aaron Black
Development Editor: James Markham
Coordinating Editor: Jessica Vakili

Distributed to the book trade worldwide by Springer Science+Business Media New York, 233 Spring Street, 6th Floor, New York, NY 10013. Phone 1-800-SPRINGER, fax (201) 348-4505, e-mail orders-ny@springer-sbm.com, or visit www.springeronline.com. Apress Media, LLC is a California LLC and the sole member (owner) is Springer Science + Business Media Finance Inc (SSBM Finance Inc). SSBM Finance Inc is a **Delaware** corporation.

For information on translations, please e-mail rights@apress.com, or visit www.apress.com/rights-permissions.

Apress titles may be purchased in bulk for academic, corporate, or promotional use. eBook versions and licenses are also available for most titles. For more information, reference our Print and eBook Bulk Sales web page at www.apress.com/bulk-sales.

Any source code or other supplementary material referenced by the author in this book is available to readers on GitHub via the book's product page, located at www.apress.com/978-1-4842-5298-7. For more detailed information, please visit www.apress.com/source-code.

Printed on acid-free paper

This book is dedicated to all those people in my family
who are no longer with us, and who died...
my grandmother Sofia, my uncle Miguel, and
my brother Polo.

Table of Contents

About the Author

Guillermo Guillen is an Electronics and Communications Engineer, and a Military Engineer. He has worked in companies as a citizen and on government projects. He is the winner of "Make with Ada 2018-19" and several prizes in three other contests. He has written this book and over 40 articles about the research, design, development, and testing of electronic equipment used in various systems with the support of AWS or other. He currently works as a micro-entrepreneur, and you can find more information at www.guillengap.com.

About the Technical Reviewer

 **Massimo Nardone** has more than 22 years of experiences in security, web/mobile development, cloud, and IT architecture. His true IT passions are security and Android. He has been programming and teaching how to program with Android, Perl, PHP, Java, VB, Python, C/C++, and MySQL for more than 20 years.

He holds a Master of Science degree in Computing Science from the University of Salerno, Italy. He has worked as a Project Manager, Software Engineer, Research Engineer, Chief Security Architect, Information Security Manager, PCI/SCADA Auditor, and Senior Lead IT Security/Cloud/SCADA Architect for many years. His technical skills include security, Android, cloud, Java, MySQL, Drupal, Cobol, Perl, web and mobile development, MongoDB, D3, Joomla, Couchbase, C/C++, WebGL, Python, Pro Rails, Django CMS, Jekyll, Scratch, etc.

He currently works as the Chief Information Security Officer (CISO) for Cargotec Oyj. He worked as a visiting lecturer and supervisor for exercises at the Networking Laboratory of the Helsinki University of Technology (Aalto University). He holds four international patents (in the PKI, SIP, SAML, and Proxy areas).

Massimo has reviewed more than 40 IT books for different publishing companies; he is the coauthor of *Pro Android Games* (Apress, 2015).

Acknowledgments

First of all, I would like to thank everyone at Apress for their help in the preparation of this book. The Apress production group has done an exceptional job in the typography and formatting of this text. The Apress professionals have always been first-class people in these projects.

I would like to thank the people of Raspberry Pi for their positive attitude towards new projects, as in my case. I have met many valuable people who have shared very useful information, especially in the discussion forums.

Thanks also to the Raspbian programmers, the Raspberry Pi operating system, which is a mix of Debian with the new Raspberry Pi desktop environment called PIXEL. The image is designed for the Pi, a machine with very discreet and powerful features.

Introduction

This book covers Python programming topics such as research, design, development, and testing of electronic devices used in the Internet of Things (IoT) and digital image processing. You don't have to be a professional programmer, but you need to have the restlessness to solve problems and use your creativity and imagination.

The first part is dedicated to the theoretical explanation of all subsequent chapters, so that you don´t get lost in some theoretical concept and miss the opportunity to understand what we are doing to solve the problem we are dealing with at that moment. I only provide you with the fundamental theoretical information; if you have the need to further expand your knowledge, I suggest you research on your own initiative in libraries and on the Internet.

In the second part of this book, you will solve problems related to the IoT. Here you will solve problems with digital ports and analog ports. Finally, you will develop a weather station in which you will put into play all your programming knowledge. You're free to solve problems and make the changes that interest you. Keep in mind that the versions of the sensors and their libraries change frequently, as do the Python and OpenCV versions, which is why I invite you to update the code on your own. Otherwise it would be impossible for me to publish this book and other materials that I intend to publish.

Finally, the last part of this book is dedicated to digital image processing, a very interesting field of programming because it´s the future of what is currently being implemented in systems dedicated to artificial intelligence. You will start by creating your own object classifier and see its advantages and disadvantages. Once you have your classifier, you will use it in applications with the Raspberry Pi camera and a webcam. You will make a robot arm with two degrees of freedom move, taking as reference the information of the coordinates (x, y) of your detected image.

CHAPTER 1

Theoretical Fundamentals

You shouldn't miss this chapter. Take it as seriously as the succeeding chapters. It's not necessary but it's highly recommended to read a book front-cover to back-cover in order to get the maximum out of it. Or to simplify things, let's put it this way: imagine this book is a movie. Now, this chapter is pretty much the first 15 minutes of the movie. You most definitely don't want to miss them!

Throughout this book, I will use Python programming, and surely you will find something new that you didn't know, so you should be clear about the concepts regardless of the level of programming you have. The Internet of Things (IoT) will be studied in Chapters 2, 3, and 4, so this is a good opportunity to know all its applications, where the imagination is the limit of what we can do. Finally, digital image processing will be studied in Chapter 5, and to understand it you must have a high capacity for abstraction, imagination, intelligence, and problem solving skills.

My general objectives for this book are as follows:

1. Without needing to be an expert in programming, you will learn to use the elements of the Python programming language to develop projects related to the IoT and digital image processing.

© Guillermo Guillen 2019
G. Guillen, *Sensor Projects with Raspberry Pi*,
https://doi.org/10.1007/978-1-4842-5299-4_1

2. You will understand and carry out IoT projects with free tools, so that you can use any service provider without problems.

3. You will carry out a digital image processing project, so that anyone can understand it and make their own proposals and code changes.

4. Most importantly, you will learn to solve problems. In all sciences not everything is solved; we only use models that hope to be debated and changed, so nobody owns the absolute truth. In a few words, there are many ways to do the same thing.

In this chapter, you will learn the basic concepts of the following topics:

- Programming the Raspberry Pi board with Python

- What the IoT is, its applications in the home, industries, and cities, and why it is used in solving technological problems

- The definition of digital image processing, methodology, techniques, and most important applications

Programming with the Raspberry Pi

Basically, Python is a language that can be used for developing anything and everything you want. Although it's an interpreted language, it's used widely because it's easier to write code and understand. If you have a manual task to automate, Python can help you do that. If you are interested in machine learning or data science, there are a bunch of awesome, well-documented libraries available for Python. Its database libraries and web development libraries are very good and are used extensively for various use cases like hosting a website.

Here are the important reasons why you should consider writing software applications in Python:

1) **Readable and maintainable code**:

   Python syntax rules allow you to express concepts without writing additional code. Python is not like other programming languages; it emphasizes code readability and allows you to use English keywords instead of punctuation. Thus, you can use Python to build custom applications without writing additional code.

2) **Compatibility with major platforms and systems**:

   Python supports many operating systems. You may even use Python interpreters to run the code on specific platforms and tools. Python also allows you to run the same code on multiple platforms without recompilation. Thus, you are not required to recompile the code after making any alteration.

3) **Robust standard library**:

   It has a large and robust standard library, making Python score over other programming languages. The standard Python library allows you to choose from a wide range of modules according to your precise needs.

4) **Many open source frameworks and tools**:

   Python, being an open source programming language, helps you to curtail software development cost significantly. You may even use several open source Python frameworks, libraries, and development tools.

Elements of the Language

As in most high-level programming languages, Python is composed of a series of elements that feed its structure, such as the following:

- Variables and constants
- Types of data
- Arithmetic operators
- Comments
- Complex data types

Variables and Constants

A variable is a space to store modifiable data in the memory of a computer. In Python, a variable is defined with the syntax

```
name_of_the_variable = value_of_the_variable
```

Each variable has a name and a value, which defines at the same time the data type of the variable. There is a type of variable called a constant that is used to define fixed values, which do not need to be modified.

Variables

Variables use descriptive and lowercase names. For compound names, you separate the words by underscores. Before and after the sign =, there must be only one blank space.

```
my_variable = 13
```

Constants

Constants use descriptive and uppercase names, separating words by underscores.

```
MY_CONSTANT = 23
```

In Python, to print a value on the screen, the word print is used.

```
my_variable = 34
print my_variable
```

The above will print the value of the variable my variable on the screen.

Types of Data

A variable or constant can contain values of various types. Consider the following examples.

Text string (string):

```
my_chain = "Hello World!"
```

Whole number:

```
age = 34
```

Octal integer:

```
age = 033
```

Hexadecimal integer number:

```
age = 0x12
```

Real number:

```
price = 745.89
```

Boolean (true/false):

```
one = True
two = False
```

There are other types of more complex data, which you will see later.

Arithmetic Operators

Among the arithmetic operators that Python uses, we can find the following:

Sum, +

```
a = 11 + 6
a is 17
```

Subtraction, –

```
a = 16 - 6
a is 10
```

Denial, –

```
a = -9
a is -9
```

Multiplication, *

```
a = 8 * 10
a is 80
```

Exponent, **

```
a = 2 ** 2
a is 4
```

Division, /

```
a = 14.4 / 2
a is 7.2
```

Integer division, //

```
a = 14.5 / 2
a is 7.0
```

Module, %

```
a = 26% 4
a is 2
```

Always place a blank before and after an operator.

Comments

A file can not only contain source code. You can also include comments or notes that explain the code better to other programmers. The comments can be of two types, single-line or multi-line, and are expressed as follows:

```
# This is a one-line comment
my_variable = 68
```

"" "And this is a comment of several lines "" "

```
my_variable = 68
my_variable = 68 # This comment  is from a line too
```

In the comments, you can include words that help identify, in addition, the subtype of comment:

```
# In the comments, you can include words that help us identify,
in addition, the subtype of comment:
```

```
# ALL this is something to do
# FIX this is something that must be corrected
```

Comments on the same line of the code must be separated with two blank spaces. Then the symbol # should go in a single blank space.

Complex Data Types

Python has, in addition to the types already seen, three more complex types, which support a collection of data. These three types can store collections of data of different types and differ in their syntax and in the way in which the data can be manipulated. These types are

- Tuples
- Lists
- Dictionaries

Tuples

A tuple is a variable that allows you to store several immutable data of different types and can´t be modified once created.

```
my_tupla = ('text string', 16, 13.8, 'other data', 78)
```

You can access each of the data by its corresponding index, with 0 (zero) as the index of the first element.

```
print my_tupla [1] # Output: 16
```

You can also access a portion of the tuple, indicating (optionally) from the start index to the end index.

```
print my_tupla [1: 4] # Returns: (16, 13.8, 'other data')
```

Another way to access the tuple in an inverse way (from back to front) is to place a negative index.

Lists

A list is similar to a tuple with the fundamental difference that it allows you to modify the data once created.

```
my_list = ['text string', 16, 13.8, 'other data', 78]
```

The lists are accessed, like the tuples, by their index number.

```
print my_list [1] # Output: 16
```

The lists are not immutable: they allow for modifying the data once created.

```
my_list [2] = 3.8 # the third element is now 3.8
```

The lists, unlike the tuples, allow adding new values.

```
my_list.append ('New Datum')
```

Dictionaries

While lists and tuples are accessed only by an index number, dictionaries allow you to use a key to declare and access a value.

```
my_dictionary = {'key_1': value_1, 'key_2': value_2, \
'key_8': value_8}
print my_dictionary ['key_2'] # Output: value_2
```

A dictionary allows you to delete any entry and, like the lists, allows you to modify the values. Python language elements are easy to understand; now let's look at control code structures.

Flow Control Structures

A control structure is a block of code that allows you to group instructions in a controlled manner. In this chapter, I will talk about two control structures:

- Conditional control structures
- Iterative control structures

Indentation

To talk about flow control structures in Python, it is essential first to talk about indentation.

What is indentation? When you write a letter, you must respect certain indentations; some computer languages require indentations too.

Not all programming languages need indentations, although they are designed to be implemented in order to grant greater readability of the source code. But in the case of Python, the indentation is mandatory, since its structure depends on it.

An indentation of four blank spaces indicates that the instructions entered are part of the same control structure.

A control structure, then, is defined as follows:

Start of the control structure:

Encoding

The encoding is another element of the language that can't be omitted when talking about control structures.

The encoding is no more than a directive that is placed at the beginning of a Python file, in order to indicate to the system the codification of characters used in the file.

```
# - * - coding: utf-8 - * -
```

utf-8 could be any character encoding. If a character encoding is not indicated, Python might fail if it encounters " strange" characters.

Multiple Assignments

Another advantage that Python provides is the ability to assign multiple variables in a single instruction.

```
a, b, c = 'string', 48, True
```

In this single instruction, I am declaring three variables, a, b, and c, and assigning a specific value to each.

```
>>> print a
string
>>> print b
48
>>> print c
True
```

The multiple assignments of variables can also be given using as values the content of a tuple.

```
>>> my_tupla = ('hello world', 2016)
>>> text, year = mi_tupla
>>> print text
hello world
>>> print year
2016
```

Or also, from a list.

```
>>> my_list = ['France', 'Paris']
>>> country, province = mi_list
>>> print country
France
>>> print provincie
Paris
```

Conditional Flow Control Structures

Conditional control structures are those that allow us to evaluate if one or more conditions are met, to say what action we are going to execute. The evaluation of conditions can only yield one of two results: true or false.

In daily life, we act according to the evaluation of conditions much more frequently than we actually believe. If the light is green, I cross the street. If it's not, I wait for the traffic light to turn green. Sometimes, we also evaluate more than one condition to execute a certain action. If the electricity bill arrives and I have money, I pay the bill.

To describe the evaluation to be performed on a condition, relational or comparison operators are used as follows:

Like, ==

```
8 == 7
False
```

Other than, !=

```
red != blue
True
```

Smaller than, <

```
8 < 77
True
```

Greater than, >

```
77 > 7
False
```

Less than or equal to, <=

```
13 <= 13
True
```

```
Greater than or equal, >=
34 >= 5
False
```

And to evaluate more than one condition simultaneously, logical operators are used:

And

```
1 == 7 and 5 < 12
0 and 0
False
```

Or

```
13 == 13 or 34 < 7
1 or 0
True
```

xor

```
45 == 45 xor 7 > 3
1 or 1
False
```

(or exclusive)

```
12 == 12 xor 10 < 3
1 or 0
True
```

The conditional flow control structures are defined by the use of three reserved keywords: if (if), elif (otherwise, yes), and else (otherwise).

Let's see an example.

```
If the traffic light is green, cross the street. If not, wait.

if semaphore == green:
    print "Cross the street"
else:
    print "Wait"
```

Iterative Control Structures

Unlike the conditional control structures, the iterative ones (also called cyclical or loops), allow us to execute the same code, repeatedly, while a condition is fulfilled.

Sometimes, we want a logical operation to be repeated several times. In Python, there are two cyclic structures available:

- while loop

- for loop

Let's review them in detail now.

While Loop

The while loop is responsible for executing the same action "while" a certain condition is met

While the year is less than or equal to 2010, print the phrase "Report of the year year".

```
# - * - coding: utf-8 - * -

year = 2002
while year <= 2010:
    print " Report of the year ", str(year)
    year += 1
```

This code will generate the following output:

```
Report of the year 2002
Report of the year 2003
Report of the year 2004
Report of the year 2005
Report of the year 2006
Report of the year 2007
Report of the year 2008
```

```
Report of the year 2009
Report of the year 2010
```

You will notice that in each iteration, we increase the value of the variable that conditions the loop (year). If we did not, this variable would always be equal to 2002 and the loop would be executed infinitely, since the condition (year <= 2010) would always be fulfilled.

But what happens if the value that conditions the iteration is not numeric and can't be increased? In that case, we can use a conditional control structure, nested within the loop, and stop the execution when the conditional stops, with the reserved keyword break:

```
while True:
    name = raw_input("What is your name? ")
    if name:
        break
```

This loop includes a nested conditional that verifies if the variable name is true and will only be true if the user types a text on the screen when the name is requested. If it is true, the loop for Sino will continue to run until the user enters a text on the screen.

For Loop

The for loop in Python is the one that will allow us to iterate over a complex variable, of the list or tuple type.

```
For each name in my_list, print name
my_list = ['John', 'Peter', 'Ana', 'Laura']
for name in my_list:
    print name
For each color in my_tupla, print color
my_tupla = ('rose', 'green', 'blue', 'yellow')
for color in my_tupla:
    print color
```

15

In these examples, name and color are two variables declared at runtime, assuming as a value that of each element of the list or tuple in each iteration.

Now that you have more programming tools, you should know that there are currently two versions of Python, so which version are you going to use?

Important Differences Between Python 2.7.x and Python 3.x

Many beginning Python users wonder which version of Python they should use. What if you are starting a new project and have the choice to pick? I would say there is currently no right or wrong choice as long as both Python 2.7.x and Python 3.x support the libraries that you are planning to use. However, it is worthwhile to have a look at the major differences between these two most popular versions of Python to avoid common pitfalls when writing the code for either one of them, or if you are planning to port your project.

Print Function

Python 2's print statement has been replaced by the print() function, meaning that we have to wrap the object that we want to print in parentheses.

Python 2 doesn't have a problem with additional parentheses, but in contrast, Python 3 will raise a syntax error if we called the print function the Python 2-way without the parentheses.

Python 3.x

```
print('Python', python_version())
print('Hello, World!')
print("some text,", end="")
print(' print more text')
```

Output

```
Python 3.4.1
Hello, World!
some text, print more text
```

In this code, the print function in Python 2.x is replaced by the print() function in Python 3.x. In other words, to print in Python 3.x an extra pair of parenthesis is required.

Division Operator

If we are porting our code or executing Python 3.x code in Python 2.x, it can be dangerous if integer division changes go unnoticed since they won't raise any errors. It is preferred to use a floating value like 6.0/5 or 6/5.0 to get the expected result when porting our code.

Python 3.x

```
print('Python', python_version())
print('3 / 2 =', 3 / 2)
print('3 // 2 =', 3 // 2)
print('3 / 2.0 =', 3 / 2.0)
print('3 // 2.0 =', 3 // 2.0)
```

Output

```
Python 3.4.1
3 / 2 = 1.5
3 // 2 = 1
3 / 2.0 = 1.5
3 // 2.0 = 1.0
```

Unicode

Python 2 has ASCII str() types, separate unicode(), but no byte type.

Now, in Python 3, we finally have Unicode (utf-8) strings, and two byte classes, byte and bytearrays.

That's to say, In Python 2, the implicit str type is ASCII. But in Python 3.x, the implicit str type is Unicode.

Python 3.x

```
print('Python', python_version())
print('strings are now utf-8 \u03BCnico\u0394é!')
Python 3.4.1
strings are now utf-8 µnicoΔé!

print('Python', python_version(), end="")
print(' has', type(b' bytes for storing data'))
Python 3.4.1 has <class 'bytes'>

print('and Python', python_version(), end="")
print(' also has', type(bytearray(b'bytearrays')))
and Python 3.4.1 also has <class 'bytearray'>
```

xrange

The xrange() of Python 2.7.x doesn't exist in Python 3.x. In Python 2.7.x, range returns a list, so range(3) returns [0, 1, 2] while xrange returns a xrange object, so xrange(3) returns an iterator object which works similar to a Java iterator and generates a number when needed.

If we need to iterate over the same sequence multiple times, it's best to use range() because it provides a static list. xrange() reconstructs the sequence every time. xrange() doesn't support slices and other list methods. The advantage of xrange() is that it saves memory when the task is to iterate over a large range.

In Python 3.x, the range function now does what xrange does in Python 2.7.x, so to keep our code portable, we should consider sticking to using range instead. So Python 3.x's range function is xrange from Python 2.7.x.

```
for x in xrange(1, 5):
    print(x),

for x in range(1, 5):
    print(x),
```

Output in Python 3.x

```
NameError: name 'xrange' is not defined
```

__future__ module

Python 3.x introduced some Python 2-incompatible keywords and features that can be imported via the built-in __future__ module in Python 2. It is recommended to use __future__ imports if you are planning Python 3.x support for your code. For example, if we want Python 3.x's integer division behavior in Python 2, we can import it via

```
from __future__ import division
```

For example, in the following Python 2.x code, we use Python 3.x's integer division behavior using __future__ module:

```
# In below python 2.7.x code, division works
# same as Python 3.x because we use __future__

from __future__ import division

print 7 / 5
print -7 / 5
```

Output

```
1.4
-1.4
```

Internet of Things

Now that you've finished with the section related to Python programming, I'll begin clarifying what the Internet of Things is and all its related topics.

Imagine a world in which every device in the home, workplace, and car is connected. A world where the lights automatically turn on when the car approaches the driveway, the coffee starts brewing when the morning alarm goes off, and the front door automatically unlocks when approached by a member of the household, but stays locked when a stranger arrives on the front step. That is the type of world the Internet of Things can create.

The true value of the Internet of Things does not lay in the lights turning on when the car reaches the driveway, but rather in the data that the connected devices collect about their users. Imagine a hospital with connected devices. The data collected from those devices outputs information on the status of patients and runs analytics on the various monitoring machines, helping the hospital to run as optimally as possible. The collection of data from devices will allow consumers, businesses, and even entire connected cities to run more efficiently. However, collecting large amounts of data presents challenges.

The IoT is the extension of Internet connectivity into physical devices and everyday objects. Embedded with electronics, Internet connectivity, and other forms of hardware such as sensors, these devices can communicate and interact with others over the Internet, and they can be remotely monitored and controlled.

The definition of the Internet of Things has evolved due to the convergence of multiple technologies, real-time analytics, machine learning, commodity sensors, and embedded systems (Figure 1-1). Traditional fields of embedded systems, wireless sensor networks, control systems, automation, and others all contribute to enabling the IoT. In the consumer market, IoT technology is most synonymous with products pertaining to the concept of the smart home, covering devices that support one or more common ecosystems and can be controlled via devices associated with that ecosystem, such as smartphones and smart speakers.

Figure 1-1. *The IoT allows objects to be controlled remotely across existing network infrastructures*

History

The concept of a network of smart devices was discussed as early as 1982, with a modified Coke vending machine at Carnegie Mellon University becoming the first Internet-connected appliance, able to report its inventory and whether newly loaded drinks were cold or not. Reza Raji described the concept in *IEEE Spectrum* as "small packets of data to a large set of nodes, so as to integrate and automate everything from home appliances to entire factories." Between 1993 and 1997, several companies proposed solutions like Microsoft at Work or Novell's NEST. The field gained momentum when Bill Joy envisioned device-to-device communication as a part of his "Six Webs" framework, presented at the World Economic Forum at Davos in 1999.

The term "Internet of Things" was likely coined by Kevin Ashton of Procter & Gamble. At that point, he viewed radio-frequency identification (RFID) as essential to the Internet of Things, which would allow computers to manage all individual things.

A research article mentioning the Internet of Things was submitted to the conference for Nordic Researchers in Norway in June 2002, which was preceded by an article published in Finnish in January 2002. The implementation is an information system infrastructure for implementing smart, connected objects.

Smart Home Applications

IoT devices are a part of the larger concept of home automation, which can include lighting, heating, and air conditioning, as well as media and security systems (Figure 1-2). Long-term benefits include energy savings by automatically ensuring lights and electronics are turned off. A smart home or automated home can be based on a platform or hubs that control smart devices. For instance, using Apple's HomeKit, manufacturers can have their home products and accessories controlled by an application on iOS devices such as the iPhone and the Apple Watch. This can be a dedicated app or iOS native applications such as Siri. There are also dedicated smart home hubs that are offered as standalone platforms to connect different smart home products; they include the Amazon Echo, Google Home, Apple's HomePod, and Samsung's SmartThings Hub.

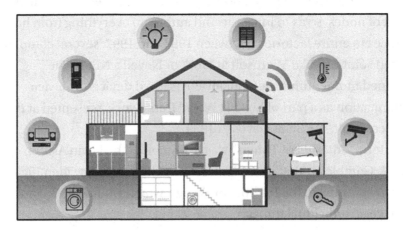

Figure 1-2. *Smart home application example*

Elder Care Applications

One key application of a smart home is to provide assistance for those with disabilities and for elderly individuals. These home systems use assistive technology to accommodate an owner's specific disabilities. Voice control can assist users with sight and mobility limitations while alert systems can be connected directly to cochlear implants worn by hearing-impaired users. They can also be equipped with additional safety features. These features can include sensors that monitor for medical emergencies such as falls or seizures. Smart home technology applied in this way can provide users with more freedom and a higher quality of life.

Medical and Healthcare Applications

The Internet of Medical Things is an application of the IoT for medical and health-related purposes, data collection and analysis for research, and monitoring. This system led to the creation of a digitized healthcare system, connecting available medical resources and healthcare services.

IoT devices can be used to enable remote health monitoring and emergency notification systems. These health monitoring devices can range from blood pressure and heart rate monitors to advanced devices capable of monitoring specialized implants, such as pacemakers, or advanced hearing aids (Figure 1-3). Some hospitals have begun implementing smart beds that can detect when they are occupied and when a patient is attempting to get up. They can also adjust to ensure appropriate pressure and support is applied to the patient without the manual interaction of nurses.

Specialized sensors can also be equipped within living spaces to monitor the health and general well-being of senior citizens, while also ensuring that proper treatment is being administered, and to help people regain lost mobility via therapy. These sensors create a network of intelligent sensors that are able to collect, process, transfer, and analyze valuable information in different environments, such as connecting in-home monitoring devices to hospital-based systems. Other consumer devices to encourage healthy living, such as connected scales or wearable heart monitors, are also a possibility with the IoT. End-to-end health monitoring IoT platforms are also available for antenatal and chronic patients, helping to manage health vitals and recurring medication requirements.

Applications have been established for point-of-care medical diagnostics, where portability and low system complexity is essential. The application of the IOT in healthcare plays a fundamental role in managing chronic diseases and in disease prevention and control. Remote monitoring is made possible through the connection of powerful wireless solutions. The connectivity enables health practitioners to capture patient's data, applying complex algorithms in health data analysis.

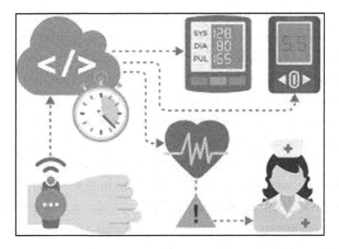

Figure 1-3. *Medical and healthcare application example*

Transportation Applications

The IoT can assist in the integration of communication, control, and information processing across various transportation systems. Application of the IoT extends to all aspects of transportation systems. Dynamic interaction between these components of a transport system enables intra-vehicular communication, smart traffic control, smart parking, electronic toll collection systems, logistics and fleet management, vehicle control, safety, and road assistance. In logistics and fleet management, for example, an IoT platform can continuously monitor the location and conditions of cargo and assets via wireless sensors and send specific alerts when management exceptions occur (Figure 1-4). This can only be possible with the IoT and its seamless connectivity among devices. Sensors such as GPS, humidity, and temperature send data to the IoT platform and then the data is analyzed and sent to the users. This way, users can track the real-time status of vehicles and can make appropriate decisions. If combined with machine learning, then it can also help in reducing traffic accidents by introducing drowsiness alerts to drivers and providing self-driven cars too.

Figure 1-4. *Transportation application example*

Building and Home Automation Applications

IoT devices can be used to monitor and control the mechanical, electrical, and electronic systems used in various types of buildings in home automation and building automation systems (Figure 1-5). In this context, three main areas are being covered in literature:

1. The integration of the Internet with building energy management systems in order to create energy efficient and IOT-driven "smart buildings."

2. The possible means of real-time monitoring for reducing energy consumption and monitoring occupant behaviors.

3. The integration of smart devices in the built environment and how they might be used in future applications.

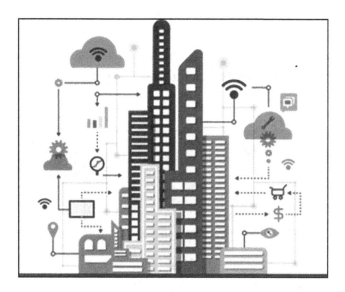

Figure 1-5. *Building and home automation application example*

Manufacturing Applications

The IoT can realize the seamless integration of various manufacturing devices equipped with sensing, identification, processing, communication, actuation, and networking capabilities. The IoT intelligent systems enable rapid manufacturing of new products, dynamic response to product demands, and real-time optimization of manufacturing production and supply chain networks, by networking machinery, sensors, and control systems together (Figure 1-6).

Digital control systems to automate process controls, operator tools, and service information systems to optimize plant safety and security are within the purview of the IoT. But it also extends to asset management via predictive maintenance, statistical evaluation, and measurements to maximize reliability. Industrial management systems can also be integrated with smart grids, enabling real-time energy optimization. Measurements, automated controls, plant optimization, health and safety management, and other functions are provided by a large number of networked sensors.

IoT in manufacturing could generate so much business value that it might eventually lead to the Fourth Industrial Revolution, also referred to as Industry 4.0.

***Figure 1-6.** Manufacturing application example*

Industrial big data analytics will play a vital role in manufacturing asset predictive maintenance, although that is not the only capability of industrial big data. Cyber-physical systems (CPS) are the core technology of industrial big data; it will be an interface between humans and the cyber world. Cyber-physical systems can be designed by following the 5C (connection, conversion, cyber, cognition, and configuration) architecture, and will transform the collected data into actionable information, and eventually interfere with the physical assets to optimize processes.

Agriculture Applications

There are numerous IoT applications in farming such as collecting data on temperature, rainfall, humidity, wind speed, pest infestation, and soil content. This data can be used to automate farming techniques, make informed decisions to improve quality and quantity, minimize risk and waste, and reduce effort required to manage crops (Figure 1-7). For example, farmers can now monitor soil temperature and moisture from afar, and even apply IoT-acquired data to precision fertilization programs.

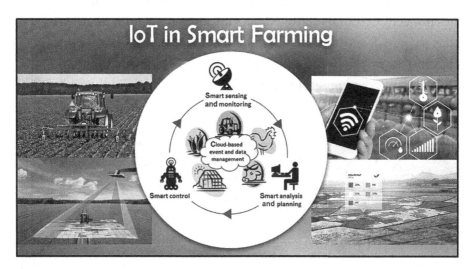

Figure 1-7. *Agriculture application example*

Metropolitan-Scale Deployments

There are several planned or ongoing large-scale deployments of the IoT to enable better management of cities and systems (Figure 1-8). For example, Songdo, South Korea, the first fully equipped and wired smart city, is gradually being built, with approximately 70 percent of the business district completed as of June 2018. Much of the city is planned to be wired and automated, with little or no human intervention.

Other examples of large-scale deployments underway include the Sino-Singapore Guangzhou Knowledge City; work on improving air and water quality, reducing noise pollution, and increasing transportation efficiency in San Jose, California; and smart traffic management in western Singapore. A French company, Sigfox, commenced building an Ultra Narrowband wireless data network in the San Francisco Bay Area in 2014, the first business to achieve such a deployment in the U.S. It subsequently announced it would set up a total of 4000 base stations to cover a total of 30 cities in the U.S. by the end of 2016, making it the largest IoT network coverage provider in the country thus far. Cisco also participates in smart cities projects. Cisco has started deploying technologies for Smart Wi-Fi, Smart Safety & Security, Smart Lighting, Smart Parking, Smart Transports, Smart Bus Stops, Smart Kiosks, and Remote Expert for Government Services (REGS) and Smart Education in the five km area in the city of Vijaywada.

Figure 1-8. *Metropolitan scale deployments example*

Energy Management Applications

Significant numbers of energy-consuming devices already integrate Internet connectivity, which allows them to communicate with utilities to balance power generation and energy usage and to optimize energy consumption as a whole. These devices allow remote control by users or central management via a cloud-based interface, and enable functions like scheduling (Figure 1-9). The smart grid is a utility-side IoT application; systems gather and act on energy and power-related information to improve the efficiency of the production and distribution of electricity. Using advanced metering infrastructure (AMI) Internet-connected devices, electric utilities not only collect data from end users, but also manage distribution automation devices like transformers.

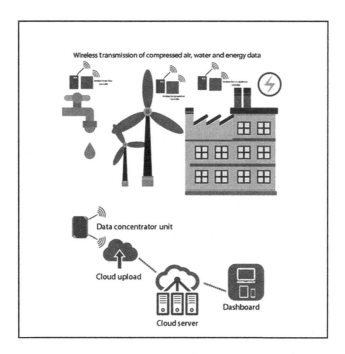

Figure 1-9. *Energy management application example*

Environmental Monitoring Applications

Environmental monitoring applications of the IoT typically use sensors to assist in environmental protection by monitoring air or water quality, atmospheric or soil conditions, and can even include areas like monitoring the movements of wildlife in their habitats (Figure 1-10). Development of resource-constrained devices connected to the Internet also means that other applications like earthquake or tsunami early-warning systems can also be used by emergency services to provide more effective aid. IoT devices in this application typically span a large geographic area and can also be mobile. It has been argued that the standardization IoT brings to wireless sensing will revolutionize this area.

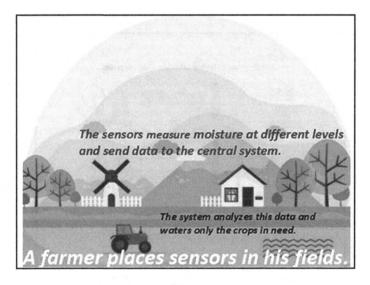

Figure 1-10. *Environmental monitoring application example*

Living Lab Application

Another example of integrating the IoT is the Living Lab, which integrates and combines research and innovative processes established within a public-private partnership (Figure 1-11). There are currently 320 Living Labs that use the IoT to collaborate and share knowledge between stakeholders to co-create innovative and technological products. For companies to implement and develop IoT services for smart cities, they need to have incentives. The governments play key roles in smart city projects as changes in policies will help cities to implement the IoT, which provides effectiveness, efficiency, and accuracy of the resources that are being used. For instance, the government provides tax incentives and cheap rent, improves public transportation, and offers an environment where start-up companies, creative industries, and multinationals may co-create, share common infrastructure and labor markets, and take advantage of locally embedded technologies, production process, and transaction costs. The relationship between the technology developers and the government that manages the city's assets is key to provide open access of resources to users in an efficient way.

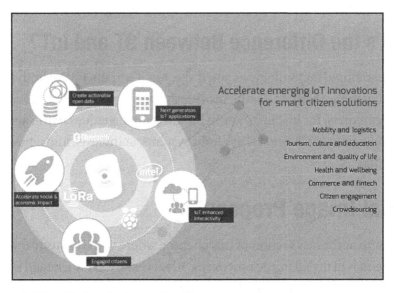

Figure 1-11. *Living Lab application example*

IoT Security

IoT security includes both physical device security and network security, encompassing the processes, technologies, and measures necessary to protect IoT devices as well as the networks they're connected to. It spans industrial machines, smart energy grids, building automation systems, employees' personal IoT devices, and more, including devices that often aren't designed for network security. IoT device security must protect systems, networks, and data from a broad spectrum of IoT security attacks, which target four types of vulnerabilities:

- Communication attacks, which put the data transmitted between IoT devices and servers at risk

- Lifecycle attacks, which put the integrity of the IoT device at risk as it changes hands from user to maintenance

- Attacks on the device software

- Physical attacks, which target the chip in the device directly

What's the Difference Between OT and IoT?

OT is operational technology, as you'll see, but it's in the mix of both that interesting things happen. Of the previously mentioned markets, IT and OT integration is, for instance, key in building management in the age of IoT. Convergence of IT and OT is about systems, standards, and a new way of thinking.

Digital Image Processing

Now you're at the last section of this chapter, where you will study the fundamentals of digital image processing. It's necessary to understand several issues: What is it? What is it for? And how has it evolved in recent years?

In computer science, digital image processing (Figure 1-12) is the use of computer algorithms to perform image processing on digital images. Essentially it improves the visual appearance, and the limitations of its applications are limited by your imagination. As a subcategory or field of digital signal processing, digital image processing has many advantages over analog image processing. It allows a much wider range of algorithms to be applied to the input data and can avoid problems such as the build-up of noise and signal distortion during processing. Since images are defined over two dimensions, digital image processing may be modeled in the form of multidimensional systems.

Figure 1-12. Digital image processing

The main advantages of digital image processing are

- Important features such as edges can be extracted from images, which can be used in industries.

- Images can be given more sharpness and better visual appearance.

- Minor errors can be rectified.

- Image sizes can be increased or decreased.

- Images can be compressed and decompressed for faster image transfer over the network.

- Images can be automatically sorted depending on their content.

- Images can be smoothened.

- It allows robots to have vision.

- It allows industries to remove defective products from the production line.

- It allows weather forecasting.

- It is used to analyze medical images.

History

Many of the techniques of digital image processing, or digital picture processing as it was often called, were developed in the 1960s at the Jet Propulsion Laboratory, Massachusetts Institute of Technology, Bell Laboratories, University of Maryland, and a few other research facilities, with application to satellite imagery, wire-photo standards conversion, medical imaging, videophone, character recognition, and photograph enhancement.

That changed in the 1970s, when digital image processing proliferated as cheaper computers and dedicated hardware became available. Images then could be processed in real time, for some dedicated problems such as television standards conversion. As general-purpose computers became faster, they started to take over the role of dedicated hardware for all but the most specialized and computer-intensive operations. With the fast computers and signal processors available in the 2000s, digital image processing has become the most common form of image processing and generally is used because it is not only the most versatile method, but also the cheapest.

Tasks

Digital image processing allows the use of much more complex algorithms, and hence can offer both more sophisticated performance at simple tasks and the implementation of methods that would be impossible by analog means. As you'll see in the following sections, digital image processing is the only practical technology.

Classification

In machine learning and statistics, classification is the problem of identifying to which of a set of categories a new observation belongs, on the basis of a training set of data containing observations whose category membership is known. Examples are assigning a given email to the "spam" or "non-spam" class, and assigning a diagnosis to a given patient based on observed characteristics of the patient. Classification is an example of pattern recognition.

Feature Extraction

Pattern recognition in machine learning and feature extraction in image processing start from an initial set of measured data and build derived values intended to be informative and non-redundant, facilitating the subsequent learning and generalization steps, and in some cases leading to better human interpretations. Feature extraction is related to dimensionality reduction. When the input data to an algorithm is too large to be processed and it is suspected to be redundant, then it can be transformed into a reduced set of features.

Multiscale Signal Analysis

Signal processing is a subfield of mathematics, computer science, information, and electrical engineering that concerns the analysis, synthesis, and modification of signals, which are broadly defined as functions conveying "information about the behavior or attributes of some phenomenon," such as sound, images, and biological measurements. For example, signal processing techniques are used to improve signal transmission fidelity, storage efficiency, and subjective quality, and to emphasize or detect components of interest in a measured signal.

Pattern Recognition

Pattern recognition is the automated recognition of patterns and regularities in data. Pattern recognition is closely related to artificial intelligence and machine learning, together with applications such as data mining and knowledge discovery in databases (KDD), and is often used interchangeably with these terms. However, they are distinguished: machine learning is one approach to pattern recognition, while other approaches include hand-crafted rules or heuristics; and pattern recognition is one approach to artificial intelligence, while other approaches include symbolic artificial intelligence.

Projection

The projection is achieved by the use of imaginary "projectors." The projected, mental image becomes the technician's vision of the desired, finished picture. By following the protocol the technician may produce the envisioned picture on a planar surface such as drawing paper. The protocols provide a uniform imaging procedure among people trained in technical graphics.

Techniques

The following sections look at some of the techniques that are used in digital image processing.

Image Editing

Image editing (Figure 1-13) encompasses the processes of altering images, whether they are digital photographs, traditional photo-chemical photographs, or illustrations. Traditional analog image editing is known as photo retouching, using tools such as an airbrush to modify photographs, or editing illustrations with any traditional art medium. Graphic software programs, which can be broadly grouped into vector graphics editors, raster graphics editors, and 3D modelers, are the primary tools with which a user may manipulate, enhance, and transform images. Many image editing programs are also used to render or create computer art from scratch.

Figure 1-13. *Image editing example*

Image Restoration

Image restoration (Figure 1-14) is the operation of taking a corrupt/noisy image and estimating the clean, original image. Corruption may come in many forms such as motion blur, noise, and camera misfocus. Image restoration is performed by reversing the process that blurred the image and as such is performed by imaging a point source and using the point source image, which is called the Point Spread Function (PSF), to restore the image information lost to the blurring process.

Figure 1-14. *Image restoration example*

Neural Networks

Artificial neural networks (ANN) or connectionist systems are computing systems that are inspired by, but not necessarily identical to, the biological neural networks that constitute animal brains. Such systems "learn" to perform tasks by considering examples, generally without being programmed with any task-specific rules. For example, in image recognition, they might learn to identify images that contain cats by analyzing example images that have been manually labeled as "cat" or "no cat" and using the results to identify cats in other images. They do this without any prior knowledge about cats, for example, that they have fur, tails, whiskers, and cat-like faces. Instead, they automatically generate identifying characteristics from the learning material that they process (Figure 1-15).

Figure 1-15. *Neural networks example*

Filtering

Digital filters are used to blur and sharpen digital images. Filtering can be performed by convolution with specifically designed kernels in the spatial domain masking specific frequency regions in the frequency domain.

To apply the affine matrix to an image, the image is converted to matrix in which each entry corresponds to the pixel intensity at that location. Then each pixel's location can be represented as a vector indicating the coordinates of that pixel in the image, [x, y], where x and y are the row and column of a pixel in the image matrix. This allows the coordinate to be multiplied by an affine-transformation matrix, which gives the position that the pixel value will be copied to in the output image.

However, to allow transformations that require translation transformations, three dimensional homogeneous coordinates are needed. The third dimension is usually set to a non-zero constant, usually 1, so that the new coordinate is [x, y, 1]. This allows the coordinate vector to be multiplied by a 3 x 3 matrix, enabling translation shifts. So the third dimension, which is the constant 1, allows translation.

Because matrix multiplication is associative, multiple affine transformations can be combined into a single affine transformation by multiplying the matrix of each individual transformation in the order that the transformations are done. This results in a single matrix that, when applied to a point vector, gives the same result as all the individual transformations performed on the vector [x, y, 1] in sequence. Thus a sequence of affine transformation matrices can be reduced to a single affine transformation matrix

Convolution

In image processing, a kernel, convolution matrix, or mask is a small matrix. It is used for blurring, sharpening, embossing, edge detection, and more. This is accomplished by doing a convolution between a kernel and an image.

The general expression of a convolution is

$$g(x,y) = \omega * f(x,y) = \sum_{s=-a}^{a} \sum_{t=-b}^{b} \omega(s,t) f(x-s,y-t),$$

where g(x,y) is the filtered image, f(x,y) is the original image, and w is the filter kernel. Every element of the filter kernel is considered by

$$-a \leq s \leq a \text{ and } -b \leq t \leq b.$$

Depending on the element values, a kernel can cause a wide range of effects (Figure 1-16).

Operation	Kernel ω	Image result g(x,y)
Identity	$\begin{bmatrix} 0 & 0 & 0 \\ 0 & 1 & 0 \\ 0 & 0 & 0 \end{bmatrix}$	
Edge detection	$\begin{bmatrix} 1 & 0 & -1 \\ 0 & 0 & 0 \\ -1 & 0 & 1 \end{bmatrix}$	
	$\begin{bmatrix} 0 & 1 & 0 \\ 1 & -4 & 1 \\ 0 & 1 & 0 \end{bmatrix}$	
	$\begin{bmatrix} -1 & -1 & -1 \\ -1 & 8 & -1 \\ -1 & -1 & -1 \end{bmatrix}$	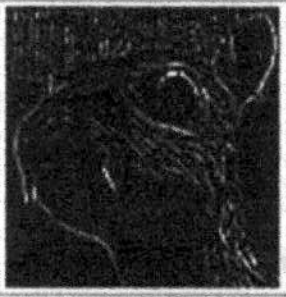
Sharpen	$\begin{bmatrix} 0 & -1 & 0 \\ -1 & 5 & -1 \\ 0 & -1 & 0 \end{bmatrix}$	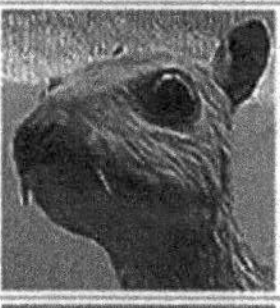
Box blur (normalized)	$\dfrac{1}{9}\begin{bmatrix} 1 & 1 & 1 \\ 1 & 1 & 1 \\ 1 & 1 & 1 \end{bmatrix}$	

Figure 1-16. *Convolution example*

Applications

After having studied a series of technical concepts in digital image processing, let's explore where these tools are used. The next two sections discuss just that.

Digital Camera Images

Digital cameras generally include specialized digital image processing hardware, either dedicated chips or added circuitry on other chips, to convert the raw data from their image sensor into a color-corrected image in a standard image file format.

Film

Westworld (1973) was the first feature film to use digital image processing to pixelate photography to simulate an android's point of view (Figure 1-17).

Figure 1-17. *Westworld, a movie that used digital image processing*

Summary

In this chapter, you learned the basic concepts of the following topics:

- Python is a widely used, general-purpose, high-level programming language. It was developed with an emphasis on code readability, and its syntax allows programmers to express concepts in fewer lines of code.

- The Internet of Things is a network in which all physical objects are connected to the Internet through network devices or routers and exchange data. The IoT allows objects to be controlled remotely across existing network infrastructures.

- Digital image processing is a method to perform some operations on an image, in order to get an enhanced image or to extract some useful information from it. It is a type of signal processing in which the input is an image and the output may be an image or features associated with that image.

In the next chapter, you will apply your knowledge of programming with Python to solve problems with the Internet of Things. You will start with simple problems and end with more complex problems.

CHAPTER 2

Alarm System

In this chapter, you'll develop an alarm system to detect the movement of someone through the use of a PIR motion sensor and the Raspberry Pi board. When this happens, you will get an alert notice through a message on your Twitter account. In this chapter, you will work exclusively with the digital ports of the Raspberry Pi to create an IoT project.

In the past, I have developed a security alarm system with Raspberry Pi and Arduino UNO, but I've never monitored the values registered in ThingSpeak and sent an alert to Twitter when the values were above a certain value. This is a good setup because we can consult the data anywhere we are without the need to directly observe the alarm system.

Hardware

A security system warns us against any external risk event such as a thief or an animal. For example, if I go out for a walk or to shop, my system, placed at my door, can detect if a strange person enters my home to steal while I am absent. I can notify the police and they can stop the thief. Another case is if I want to hunt a mouse in my home. This system can detect when the mouse prowls in front of the sensor and notify me through the IoT system. I can hunt it if my mousetrap fails.

This project offers very good advantages, as you can see in Figure 2-1. This project is economical, consumes little energy, uses a Raspberry Pi board, and can be modified according to your needs.

© Guillermo Guillen 2019
G. Guillen, *Sensor Projects with Raspberry Pi*,
https://doi.org/10.1007/978-1-4842-5299-4_2

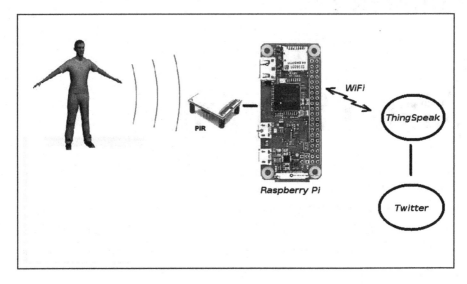

Figure 2-1. *Alarm system schematic diagram*

It works as follows:

1. The PIR motion sensor uses infrared signals to detect the presence of a person (Figure 2-1).

2. Immediately after, and through the WiFi connection of the Raspberry Pi board, it connects to a remote server called ThingSpeak where this data system is stored.

3. When the system detects the movement of a person, the system sends a logical 1 to the ThingSpeak server; when there is nothing, a logical 0 is sent.

4. When a logical 1 is detected in the database, ThingSpeak activates an alert automatically.

5. The alert creates a message that is sent to your Twitter account.

6. You can check the message and the time it was sent to your Twitter account either on your computer or on your cell phone or smart phone.

This is an economical way to have a security system in your home without spending a lot of money. The hardware costs less than $25 USD and you can use a free IoT service provider (but you may be limited in the number of channels). If you need more than four channels, you may have to spend $5-10 a month. Remember that in each channel you can monitor a single sensor, so if you put five sensors in your house, you need five channels. You can use magnetic sensors or switches on your doors and windows, and connect them directly to the security system without any difficulty.

Remember that the PIR motion sensor can be powered with 3 or 5 volts CD. Its output is 3 volts of CD, so it is compatible with the Raspberry board (Figure 2-2).

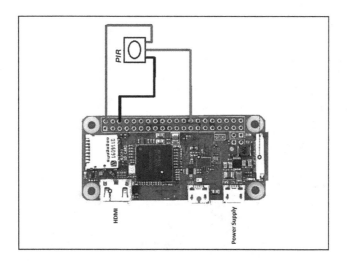

Figure 2-2. *Alarm system electronic diagram*

The following are all of the parts needed for this project:

- Raspberry Pi Zero W

- PIR motion sensor

The project looks like Figures 2-3 and 2-4.

Figure 2-3. *Test with the system*

Figure 2-4. *Top view*

Now that you have assembled the circuit, you must program the Raspberry Pi board. If you have any questions regarding the identification of the pins of the hardware, please consult the appendix.

Software

The complete source code and libraries can be found at

https://drive.google.com/file/d/1850gMBb-iTPqcYTLT-bREXNo6uDuk9SH/view?usp=sharing.

I've added comments here to better explain what the code is doing. They are marked by # and do not need to be reproduced when entering the code.

```
//******************************

# Import required Python libraries
import sys
import RPi.GPIO as GPIO
import os
import time
from time import sleep
import urllib2

# Use BCM GPIO references
# instead of physical pin numbers
GPIO.setmode(GPIO.BCM)

# Define GPIO to use on Pi
GPIO_PIR = 7

print "PIR Module Test (CTRL-C to exit)"

# Set pin as input
GPIO.setup(GPIO_PIR,GPIO.IN)      # Echo
```

```
#Setup our API and delay
myAPI = "OVD5H5HULC90XH27"  # API Key from thingSpeak.com channel
myDelay = 15 #how many seconds between posting data

def getSensorData():
    Current_State  = 0
    Previous_State = 0
    PIR = 0
    try:

        # Loop until users quits with CTRL-C
        while True :
            # Read PIR state
            Current_State = GPIO.input(GPIO_PIR)

            if Current_State==1 and Previous_State==0:
                    # PIR is triggered
                    print "  Motion detected!"
                    # Record previous state
                    Previous_State=1
                    PIR = 1
            elif Current_State==0 and Previous_State==1:
                    # PIR has returned to ready state
                    print "  Ready2"
                    Previous_State=0
                    PIR = 0
            return (str(PIR))

    except KeyboardInterrupt:
        print "  Quit"
        # Reset GPIO settings
        GPIO.cleanup()
```

```python
def main():
    print 'starting...'
    baseURL = 'https://api.thingspeak.com/update?api_key=%s'
            % myAPI
    print baseURL
    while True:
        try:
            print "Reading Sensor Data now"
            PIR = getSensorData()
            print PIR + " "
            f = urllib2.urlopen(baseURL + "&field1=%s" % (PIR))
            print f.read()
            f.close()
            sleep(int(myDelay))
        except Exception as e:
            print e
            print 'exiting.'
            break

if __name__ == '__main__':
    main()
//*****************************
```

It's important to note that you must replace the Write API key on line 22 where it says "My API" in bold with the one that you created in the ThingSpeak server.

You start by connecting to your ThingSpeak account and using the Write API key that the server generated. You then read the data captured by the PIR motion sensor. Finally, you send the data to the server of ThingSpeak and wait 15 seconds to start over again.

Procedure

To use the tools of the IoT service provider, you must follow the guidelines indicated. I'll show you how to fill out the reports. There may be some changes by the time you read this; however, the actions are the same.

Creating a Project in ThingSpeak

The next step is to create an account at `https://thingspeak.com`.

You are ready to create a new channel, so add the following data, as shown in Figure 2-5:

> Name: Alarm System
>
> Description: Sensors: PIR
>
> Field1: PIR

Channel Settings

Percentage complete	50%
Channel ID	500490
Name	Alarm System
Description	Sensors: PIR
Field 1	PIR ☑
Field 2	☐
Field 3	☐
Field 4	☐
Field 5	☐
Field 6	☐
Field 7	☐
Field 8	☐
Metadata	

Figure 2-5. *Fill out this form for channel configuration*

Save the project. The system will provide you with the channel number and the Write API key.

Copy the Write API key, which is 16 characters, and paste it into the Python code where it says

```
myAPI = "GET_YOUR_KEY"
```

The result is shown in Figure 2-6. Remember that in the free account in ThingSpeak you can only monitor a maximum of four channels simultaneously.

55

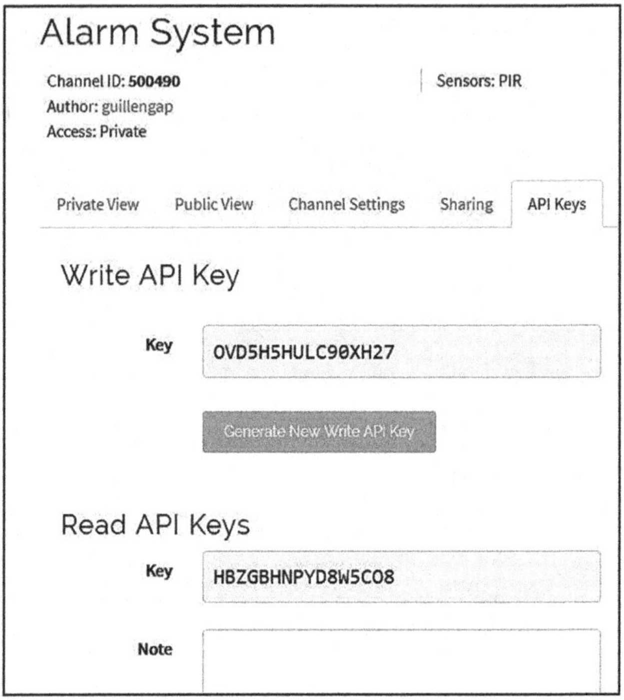

Alarm System

Channel ID: **500490**   Sensors: PIR
Author: guillengap
Access: Private

Private View   Public View   Channel Settings   Sharing   API Keys

Write API Key

Key   OVD5H5HULC90XH27

Generate New Write API Key

Read API Keys

Key   HBZGBHNPYD8W5CO8

Note

Figure 2-6. *Take note of the Write API key*

When your project is working on the IoT server, you can watch
something similar to Figure 2-7.

Figure 2-7. *Graph drawn on the ThingSpeak server*

Using Your Twitter Account in ThingSpeak

Click Apps and then click ThingTweet (Figure 2-8). Link your Twitter account and the system will provide you with an API key (Figure 2-9).

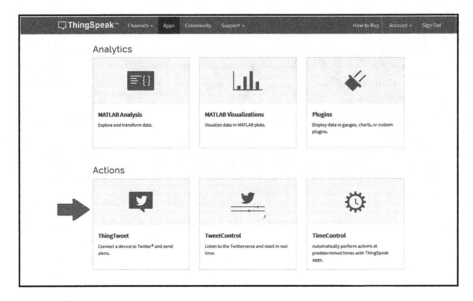

Figure 2-8. *In Analytics, select ThingTweet*

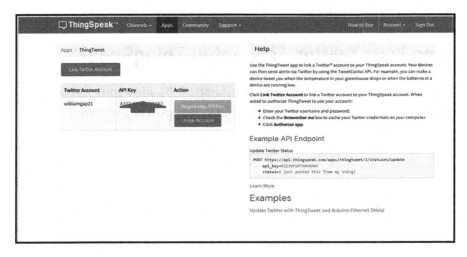

Figure 2-9. *Take note of the API key*

Sending an Alert to Your Twitter Account

Click Apps and then click React, as shown in Figure 2-10.

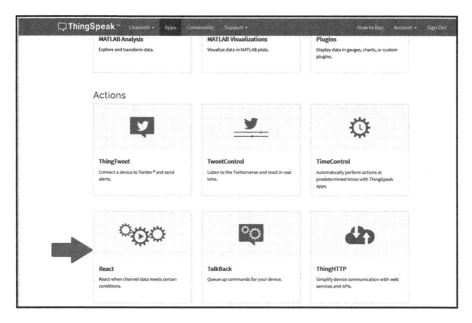

Figure 2-10. *Remember that the versions of ThingSpeak can change and you must understand what we are doing*

Now create a new React. The system will ask you to fill in the data shown in Figure 2-11 for the PIR motion sensor.

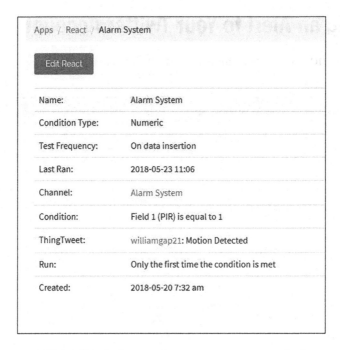

Apps / React / Alarm System

Edit React

Name:	Alarm System
Condition Type:	Numeric
Test Frequency:	On data insertion
Last Ran:	2018-05-23 11:06
Channel:	Alarm System
Condition:	Field 1 (PIR) is equal to 1
ThingTweet:	williamgap21: Motion Detected
Run:	Only the first time the condition is met
Created:	2018-05-20 7:32 am

Figure 2-11. *Fill in this information so you can send alerts to your Twitter account on every first occasion that field 1 equals 1*

You should see something like Figure 2-12 in your Twitter account.

Tweets   Tweets y respuestas   Multimedia

Guillermo Guillen @williamgap21 · 1 h
Motion Detected

Figure 2-12. *The alert sent by the ThingSpeak server to my Twitter account*

Challenges

You can work with digital ports using the Hall Effect sensor, switches, or infrared sensors.

Conclusion

You learned that digital ports can be enabled to transmit control data in an IoT system. The tests performed were satisfactory with the PIR motion sensor. There was no error.

CHAPTER 3

Gas Leak Alarm

In this chapter, you'll develop a system for the detection of fires or gas leaks with the Raspberry Pi board and the MQ2 gas sensor. This system will send the captured data to the remote ThingSpeak server and, when a gas increase is detected beyond a programed limit, send a message to your Twitter account. In this project, you'll use an analog port and the IoT ThingSpeak server.

I have developed a gas leak alarm with a microcontroller before but I have never monitored the values registered in ThingSpeak and sent an alert to Twitter when the values were above a certain level, so this is a good experience. You can check this data anywhere you are without the need to directly observe the MQ2 gas sensor.

Hardware

Let's begin by making the electrical connections shown in Figure 3-1. The following electronic components are shown in Figure 3-1:

- Raspberry Pi Zero W

- ADS1115

- MQ2 gas sensor

- Resistor 10k

© Guillermo Guillen 2019
G. Guillen, *Sensor Projects with Raspberry Pi*,
https://doi.org/10.1007/978-1-4842-5299-4_3

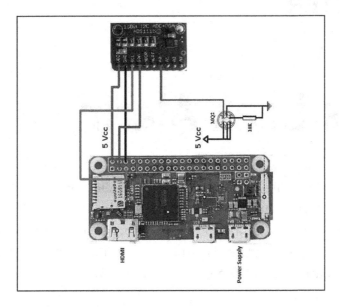

Figure 3-1. *Electrical diagram*

Use the ADS1115 digital-analog converter to interface the MQ2 gas sensor with the Raspberry Pi board. To do so, you must install the library of this device and you must activate the 12C interface. You can download the library from the link at the end of this tutorial.

You can install from pip with

```
$ sudo pip install adafruit-ads1x15
```

Remember that Unix language knowledge is required. Alternatively, to install the library from source (recommended), run the following commands on the Raspberry Pi system:

```
$ sudo apt-get install git build-essential python-dev
$ cd ~
$ git clone https://github.com/adafruit/Adafruit_Python_ADS1x15.git
$ cd Adafruit_Python_ADS1x15
$ sudo python setup.py install
```

You must activate the 12C interface on the Raspberry Pi Configuration screen and reboot the system to work correctly, as shown in Figure 3-2.

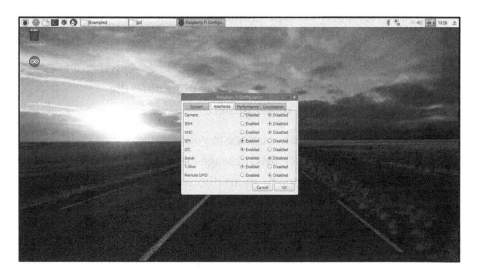

Figure 3-2. *Activation of the 12C interface*

The ADS1115 digital-analog converter can be configured for 16 and 15 bits. In this case, you are going to use the 16 bits and for this the following instruction is configured in code:

```
GAIN = 1
```

In Figure 3-3, you can see that the MQ2 gas sensor detects the presence of fire and LP gas, and then the Raspberry Pi board connects to the remote ThingSpeak server to capture them. The ThingSpeak server, in turn, sends an alert to your Twitter account.

Here's a snapshot of how it works:

1. The gas leak is detected by the MQ2 gas sensor.

2. This sensor is analog and its output has to pass through the analog-to digital-converter, ADS1115, which is set to 16 bits; that is, it samples from 0 to 32768 quantization values.

3. The ADS1115 device connects to the SCL and SDA pins on the Raspberry Pi board.

4. The Raspberry Pi board connects via your WiFi to the remote ThingSpeak server and sends the captured data of your analog port A0.

5. If the captured data exceeds 12000 units, then the ThingSpeak server sends an alert.

6. The alert is sent via a message to your Twitter account. You can see this message either on your PC or on your cell phone or smart phone.

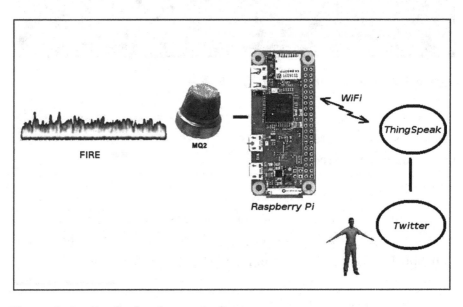

Figure 3-3. *Gas leak schematic diagram*

The project looks like Figures 3-4 and 3-5.

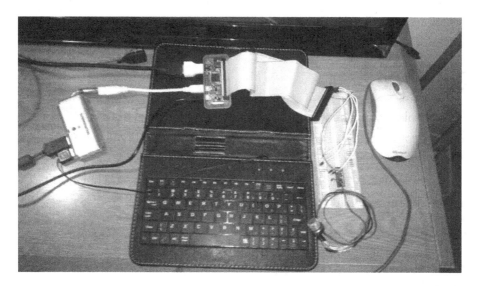

Figure 3-4. *Complete system in operation*

Figure 3-5. *MQ2 gas sensor*

Now that you have seen how to connect the hardware of your system, the next step is to program your Raspberry Pi board. If you have any questions regarding the hardware pins used, please consult the appendix.

Software

The complete source code and libraries can be found at https://drive.google.com/file/d/11iq8Mjo4z_QZhoj2HpTqQlfg4GwoIt6n/view?usp=sharing.

Comments have been added here and are marked by #. They don't need to be reproduced when entering the code.

```
//*****************************

# Import required Python libraries
import sys
import os
import time
from time import sleep
import urllib2
import Adafruit_ADS1x15

# Create an ADS1115 ADC (16-bit) instance.
adc = Adafruit_ADS1x15.ADS1115()

GAIN = 1

#Setup our API and delay
myAPI = "OICJL711JK2CON1H"  # API Key from thingSpeak.com channel
myDelay = 15 #how many seconds between posting data

def getSensorData():
```

```
MQ2 = 0
print('Reading ADS1x15 values, press Ctrl-C to quit...')
# Print nice channel column headers.
print('| {0:>6} | {1:>6} | {2:>6} | {3:>6} |'.format(*range(4)))
print('-' * 37)

try:

    # Main loop until users quits with CTRL-C
    while True :
        # Read all the ADC channel values in a list.
        values = [0]*4
        for i in range(4):
                # Read the specified ADC channel using the
                  previously set gain value.
                values[i] = adc.read_adc(i, gain=GAIN)
                MQ2 = values[0]
        # Print the ADC values.
        print('| {0:>6} | {1:>6} | {2:>6} | {3:>6}
        |'.format(*values))
        return (str(MQ2))

except KeyboardInterrupt:
    print "  Quit"

def main():
    print 'starting...'
    baseURL = 'https://api.thingspeak.com/update?api_key=%s' % myAPI
    print baseURL
    while True:
        try:
            print "Reading Sensor Data now"
            MQ2 = getSensorData()
```

```
            print MQ2 + " "
            f = urllib2.urlopen(baseURL + "&field1=%s" % (MQ2))
            print f.read()
            f.close()
            sleep(int(myDelay))
        except Exception as e:
            print e
            print 'exiting.'
            break

if __name__ == '__main__':
    main()
```

//****************************

Note that you must replace the write API key on line 22 (shown in bold) with the one you created for the ThingSpeak server. Follow the steps provided in Chapter 2 to generate the code. You can also find good examples in the IC ADS115 library to understand how it works.

To use the tools of the IoT service provider, you must follow the guidelines indicated.

Procedure

Now it's time to fill out the reports.

Installing the ADS1115 Sensor Library

The ADS1115 library is attached at the end of this tutorial and is called Adafruit_Python_ADS1x15-master.zip.

Unzip the package. To execute the installation, type the following in the command line:

```
>>> sudo python setup.py install
```

In the library you can find simple examples to test the ADS1115 sensor (Figure 3-6).

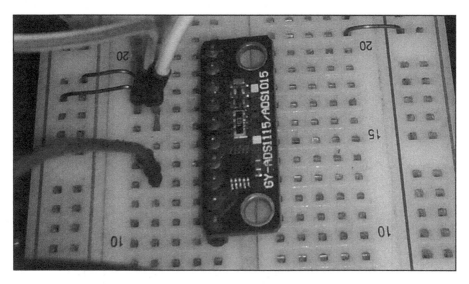

Figure 3-6. *ADS1115 board*

Enabling the 12C Interface

You must activate the 12C interface on the Raspberry Pi Configuration screen and reboot the system to work correctly. Go to Menu ➤ Preferences ➤ Raspberry Pi Configuration.

Creating a Project in ThingSpeak

Use the ThingSpeak account you created in Chapter 2 and create a new channel with the following data (Figure 3-7):

Name: Gas Leak Alarm

Description: Alarm System with MQ2 gas sensor

Field1: MQ2

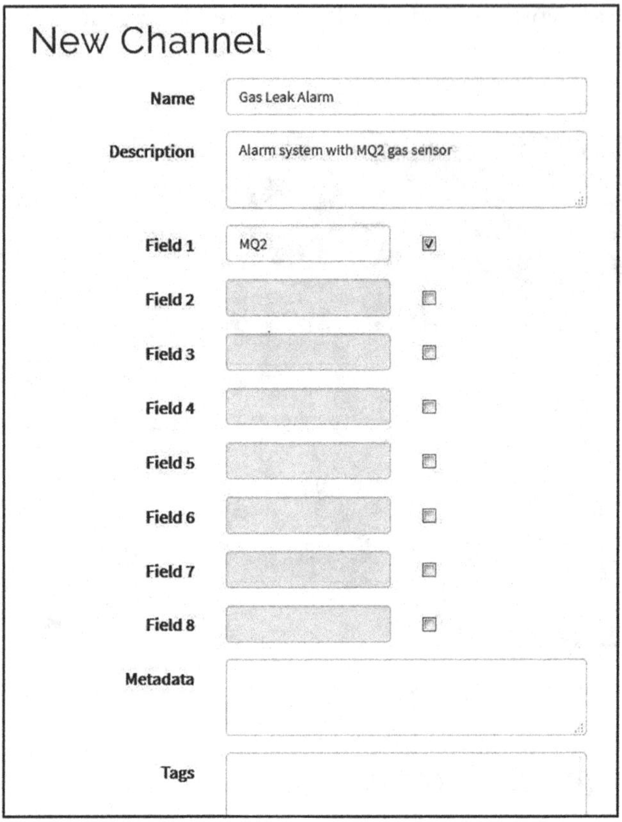

Figure 3-7. *Creating a new channel*

Save the project. The system will provide you with the channel number and the Write API key (Figure 3-8).

Copy the Write API key, which is 16 characters, and paste it into the Python code where it says

```
myAPI = "GET_YOUR_KEY"
```

Remember that in the free account in ThingSpeak you can only monitor a maximum of four channels simultaneously.

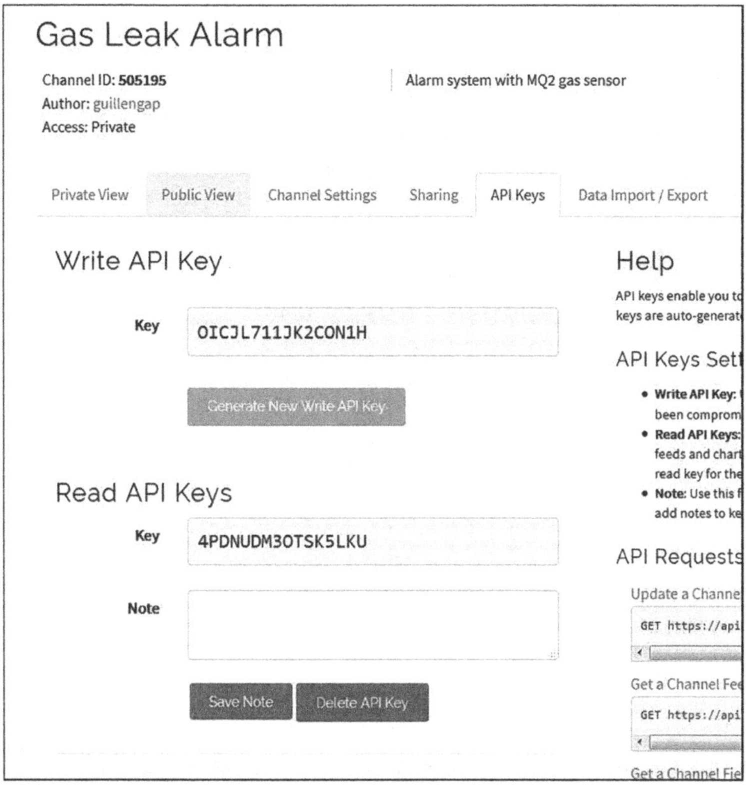

Figure 3-8. *Getting the Write API key*

Figures 3-9 and 3-10 show how the system works. In Figure 3-9, the sensor measures the amount of gas in the environment and sends the data to the IoT server. In Figure 3-10, the IoT server plots the data it is receiving on a channel.

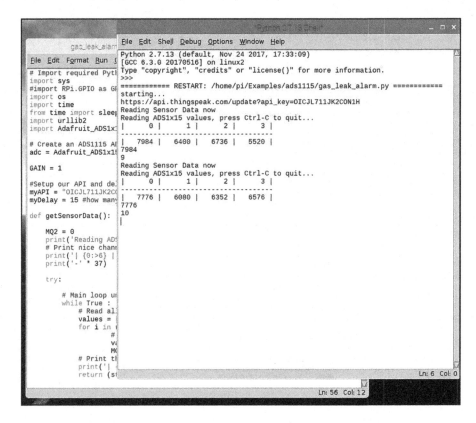

Figure 3-9. *Data sent by the Raspberry Pi board to the ThingSpeak server*

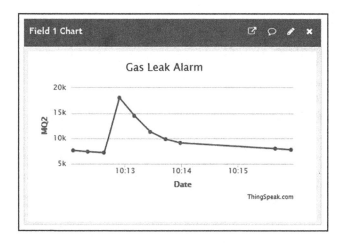

Figure 3-10. *Graph in the ThingSpeak server*

Using Your Twitter Account in ThingSpeak

To use your Twitter account in ThingSpeak, follow the instructions provided in Chapter 2.

Sending an Alert to Your Twitter Account

Click Apps and then click React. Create a new React and fill in the data shown in Figure 3-11.

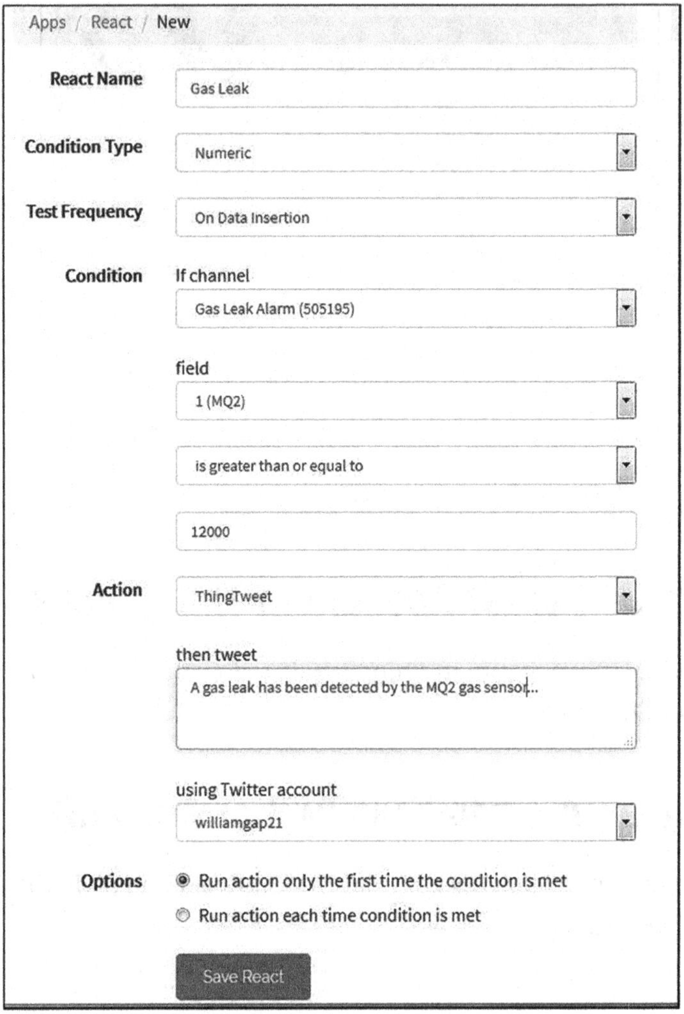

Figure 3-11. *Fill out this react*

At the end, you will have the data shown in Figure 3-12.

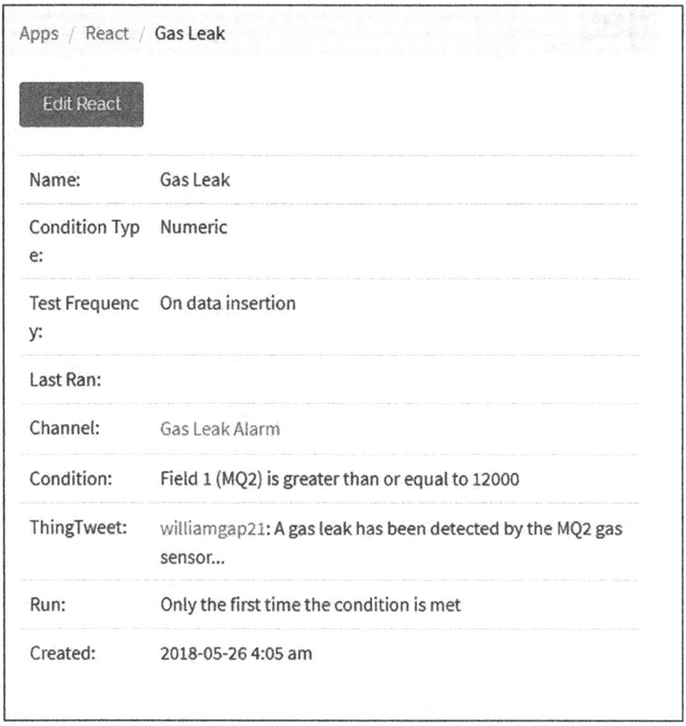

Apps / React / Gas Leak

Edit React

Name:	Gas Leak
Condition Type:	Numeric
Test Frequency:	On data insertion
Last Ran:	
Channel:	Gas Leak Alarm
Condition:	Field 1 (MQ2) is greater than or equal to 12000
ThingTweet:	williamgap21: A gas leak has been detected by the MQ2 gas sensor...
Run:	Only the first time the condition is met
Created:	2018-05-26 4:05 am

Figure 3-12. *Finishing the react*

You can see an example of a tweet alert in Figure 3-13.

Tweets   Tweets y respuestas   Multimedia

Guillermo Guillen @williamgap21 · 57 min
A gas leak has been detected by the MQ2 gas sensor...

🌐 Traducir Tweet

💬   ↻   ♡   �

Figure 3-13. *Alert sent by the ThingSpeak server to my Twitter account*

Challenges

Using analog ports, experiment with a TMP36 temperature sensor or LDR sensor.

Conclusion

In this chapter, you made use of the analog ports of the ADS1115 integrated circuit to send analog MQ2 sensor data to the Raspberry Pi board. This board sent the data to the ThingSpeak IoT server.

CHAPTER 4

Weather Station

The main goal of this project is to develop a weather station with Raspberry Pi and to be able to monitor all the sensors with ThingSpeak and Twitter. The sensors used without any problems are the DHT11 (humidity and temperature sensor) and the BMP085 (barometric pressure and temperature sensor).

Why not use the DHT22, BMP180, or the BMP280? The reasons are because the manufacturers are always going to come out with new versions of these sensors and I'd never finish this chapter and book. Don't worry; the adjustments will be minimal between one sensor version and another.

A weather station is a facility, either on land or sea, with instruments and equipment for measuring atmospheric conditions to provide information for weather forecasts and to study the climate. The measurements taken include temperature, atmospheric pressure, humidity, wind speed, wind direction, and precipitation amounts. Wind measurements are taken with as few other obstructions as possible, while temperature and humidity measurements are kept free from direct solar radiation or insulation. Manual observations are taken at least once a day, while automated measurements are taken at least once an hour. In this chapter, you will limit yourself to measuring humidity, temperature, barometric pressure, and height above sea level.

© Guillermo Guillen 2019
G. Guillen, *Sensor Projects with Raspberry Pi*,
https://doi.org/10.1007/978-1-4842-5299-4_4

Hardware

Make the electrical connections of the diagram in Figure 4-1.

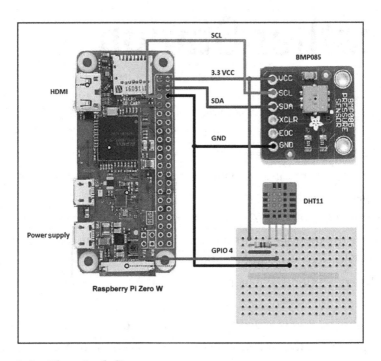

Figure 4-1. *Electrical diagram*

The barometric pressure sensor BMP085 is used to measure the atmospheric pressure between 300 and 1100hPa. It can also measure between -500 and 9000 meters above sea level, making the corresponding calculations. Additionally, it measures the temperature from 0 to 65 degrees centigrade. You must activate the 12C interface on the Raspberry Pi Configuration screen and reboot the system for it to work correctly. You can download the library from the link provided at the end of this tutorial.

The DHT11 sensor measures the relative humidity between 20% and 90%; it also measures the temperature between 0 and 50 degrees Celsius. The digital output is through a simple signal bus.

When the communication between the application and the Raspberry Pi board is established, you can perform the following functions in an interactive way:

1. The sensors begin to work and perform the tasks that correspond to them.

2. The DHT11 sensor measures the relative humidity and temperature in degrees Celsius and sends the data to the Raspberry Pi board.

3. The BMP085 sensor sends the barometric pressure data in hPa and the temperature in degrees Celsius to the Raspberry Pi board. Here you make the conversion to mmHg.

4. You print the measured values on the screen.

5. You send the following measured values to the ThingSpeak server: temperature measured by the DHT11 sensor, humidity measured by the DHT11 sensor, pressure measured in mmHg by the BMP085 sensor, and height calculated by the BMP085 sensor.

6. The ThingSpeak server sends a ThingTweet when the temperature is above 25 degrees Celsius and another ThingTweet when the humidity is above 45%.

The following are the parts needed for this project:

- Raspberry Pi Zero W

- DHT11 humidity sensor

- BMP085 barometric pressure sensor

- Resisitor 4k7

Figures 4-2 through 4-5 show this project.

Figure 4-2. *Testing the weather station*

Figure 4-3. *Top view with sensors DHT11 and BMP085*

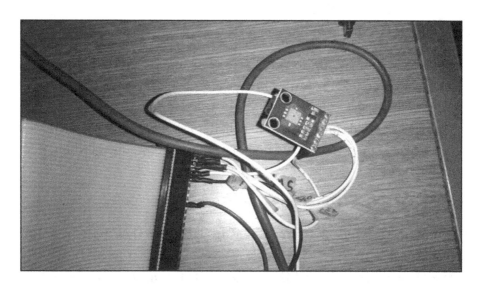

Figure 4-4. *BMP085 barometric pressure sensor*

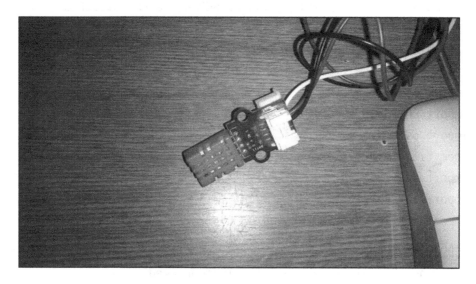

Figure 4-5. *DHT11 humidity sensor*

83

Software

The complete source code and libraries can be found at https://
drive.google.com/file/d/1QPtOBx8qhAONMWuOkrrJI--6M86ZPoZE/
view?usp=sharing.

Here, I've added comments here to better explain what the code is
doing. They are marked by # and do not need to be reproduced when
entering the code.

```
//*******************************

# Script will be used to read sensor data and then post the IoT
  Thinkspeak
# Read Temperature & Humidity using DHT11 sensor attached to
  Raspberry PI Zero W
# Read Pressure and Altitude using BMP085 sensor attached to
  Raspberry PI Zero W
# Program posts these values to a thingspeak channel
# Import all the libraries we need to run
import sys
import RPi.GPIO as GPIO
import os
from time import sleep
import Adafruit_DHT
import urllib2
import Adafruit_BMP.BMP085 as BMP085

DEBUG = 1
# Define GPIO pin to which DHT11 is connected
DHTpin = 4
#Setup our API and delay
myAPI = " GET_YOUR_KEY"  # API Key from thingSpeak.com channel
myDelay = 15 #how many seconds between posting data
```

```python
GPIO.setmode(GPIO.BCM)

def getSensorData():
    print "In getSensorData";
    humidity, temperature = Adafruit_DHT.read_retry(Adafruit_
    DHT.DHT11, DHTpin)
    sensor = BMP085.BMP085()
    if humidity is not None and temperature is not None:
        print('Temp={0:0.1f}*C  Humidity={1:0.1f}%'.format
        (temperature, humidity))
        TWF=((9.0/5*temperature)+32)
        print('TempF={0:0.1f}*F'.format(TWF))
#        print('Temp = {0:0.2f} *C'.format(sensor.read_
         temperature()))
        Pressure = sensor.read_pressure()
        Altitude = sensor.read_altitude()
        print('Pressure = {0:0.2f} Pa'.format(sensor.read_
        pressure()))
        print('Altitude = {0:0.2f} m'.format(sensor.read_
        altitude()))
    else:
        print('Failed to get reading. Try again!')
    return (str(humidity), str(temperature), str(Pressure),
    str(Altitude))

def main():
    print 'starting...'
    baseURL = 'https://api.thingspeak.com/update?api_key=%s'
    % myAPI
    print baseURL
    while True:
        try:
```

```
                print "Reading Sensor Data now"
                RHW, TW, Pressure, Altitude = getSensorData()
                print TW + " " + RHW + " " + Pressure + " " + Altitude + " "

                f = urllib2.urlopen(baseURL + "&field1=%s&field2=
                    %s&field3=%s&field4=%s" % (TW, RHW, Pressure,
                    Altitude))
                print f.read()
                f.close()
                sleep(int(myDelay))
        except Exception as e:
            print e
            print 'exiting.'
            break

# call main

if __name__ == '__main__':
    main()

//*****************************
```

Here is an example of what to do if you use another sensor. If you use the BMP180 sensor, download the library for this sensor, and change the following line:

```
import Adafruit_BMP.BMP180 as BMP180
```

Also, change the next line of code:

```
sensor = BMP180.BMP180 ()
```

Many of your doubts will be eased when you test the sensors. For example, I suggest you try the DHT humidity sensor with this example from the library:

AdafruitDHT.py

```
//*****************************

import sys

import Adafruit_DHT

# Parse command line parameters.
sensor_args = { '11': Adafruit_DHT.DHT11,
                '22': Adafruit_DHT.DHT22,
                '2302': Adafruit_DHT.AM2302 }
if len(sys.argv) == 3 and sys.argv[1] in sensor_args:
    sensor = sensor_args[sys.argv[1]]
    pin = sys.argv[2]
else:
    print('usage: sudo ./Adafruit_DHT.py [11|22|2302] GPIOpin#')
    print('example: sudo ./Adafruit_DHT.py 2302 4 - Read from
    an AM2302 connected to GPIO #4')
    sys.exit(1)

# Try to grab a sensor reading.  Use the read_retry method
  which will retry up
# to 15 times to get a sensor reading (waiting 2 seconds
  between each retry).
humidity, temperature = Adafruit_DHT.read_retry(sensor, pin)

# Un-comment the line below to convert the temperature to
  Fahrenheit.
# temperature = temperature * 9/5.0 + 32

# Note that sometimes you won't get a reading and
# the results will be null (because Linux can't
# guarantee the timing of calls to read the sensor).
# If this happens try again!
if humidity is not None and temperature is not None:
```

```
    print('Temp={0:0.1f}*  Humidity={1:0.1f}%'.format
    (temperature, humidity))
else:
    print('Failed to get reading. Try again!')
    sys.exit(1)
```

//*****************************

For sensor BMP085, you can test it with the following code:
Simpletest.py

//*****************************

```
import Adafruit_BMP.BMP085 as BMP085

# Default constructor will pick a default I2C bus.
#
# For the Raspberry Pi this means you should hook up to the
  only exposed I2C bus
# from the main GPIO header and the library will figure out the
  bus number based
# on the Pi's revision.
# For the Beaglebone Black the library will assume bus 1 by
  default, which is
# exposed with SCL = P9_19 and SDA = P9_20.
sensor = BMP085.BMP085()

# Optionally you can override the bus number:
#sensor = BMP085.BMP085(busnum=2)

# You can also optionally change the BMP085 mode to one of
  BMP085_ULTRALOWPOWER,
# BMP085_STANDARD, BMP085_HIGHRES, or BMP085_ULTRAHIGHRES.  See
  the BMP085
```

```
# datasheet for more details on the meanings of each mode
  (accuracy and power
# consumption are primarily the differences).  The default mode
  is STANDARD.
#sensor = BMP085.BMP085(mode=BMP085.BMP085_ULTRAHIGHRES)

print('Temp = {0:0.2f} *C'.format(sensor.read_temperature()))
print('Pressure = {0:0.2f} Pa'.format(sensor.read_pressure()))
print('Altitude = {0:0.2f} m'.format(sensor.read_altitude()))
print('Sealevel Pressure = {0:0.2f} Pa'.format(sensor.read_
sealevel_pressure()))

//*****************************
```

Now that you have assembled the hardware pieces and you've programmed your Raspberry Pi board, you may have some problems with the installation of the libraries or with the configuration of the IoT server. This is what the next section is about.

Procedure

In the following sections, you will correctly install the libraries and also learn to configure the IoT server. Remember that in the previous chapters you used analog and digital sensors, but now you are using sensors with the 12C protocol interface from different manufacturers.

Installing the DHT11 Sensor Library

The DHT11 moisture sensor library is attached at the end of this tutorial and is called Adafruit_Python_DHT-master.zip.

Optionally, you can download the library from https://github.com/adafruit/Adafruit_Python_DHT.git.

Unzip the package. To execute the installation, type the following in the command line:

```
>>> sudo python setup.py install
```

In the library you can find simple examples to test this sensor.

Installing the BMP085 Sensor Library

The BMP085 pressure sensor library is attached at the end of this tutorial and is called Adafruit_Python_BMP-master.zip.

Optionally, you can download the library from

https://github.com/adafruit/Adafruit_Python_BMP.

Unzip the package. To execute the installation, type the following in the command line:

```
>>> sudo python setup.py install
```

In the library you can find simple examples to test this sensor.

Enabling the 12C Interface

You must activate the 12C interface on the Raspberry Pi Configuration screen and reboot the system for it to work correctly.

Creating a Project in ThingSpeak

Use the account you created earlier and create a new channel. Enter the following data (Figure 4-6):

Name: WeatherStation

Description:

Field1: Temperature (C)

Field2: Humidity (%)

Field3: Pressure (hPa)

Field4: Altitude (m)

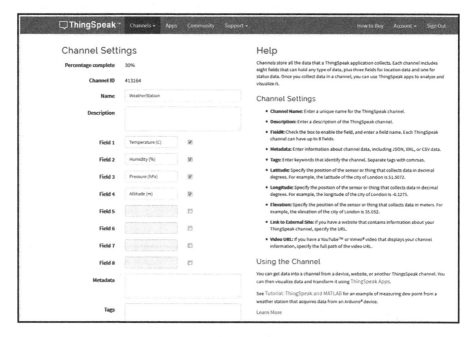

Figure 4-6. *Creating a new channel*

Save the project. The system will provide you with the channel number and the Write API key.

Copy the Write API key, which is 16 characters, and paste it into the Python code where it says

```
myAPI = "GET_YOUR_KEY"
```

Remember that in the free account in ThingSpeak you can only monitor a maximum of four channels simultaneously.

91

With this configuration, you can get the information shown in Figures 4-7 through 4-11.

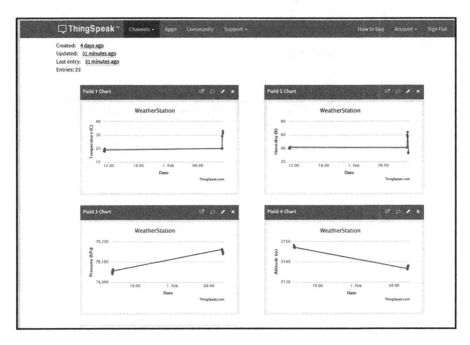

Figure 4-7. *Four graphs on the ThingSpeak server*

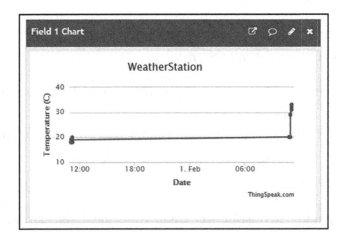

Figure 4-8. *Temperature graph*

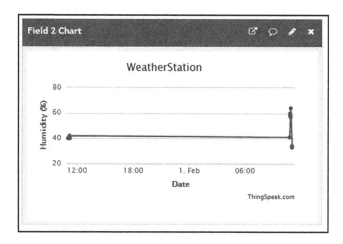

Figure 4-9. *Humidity graph*

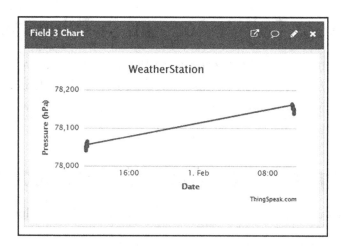

Figure 4-10. *Pressure graph*

93

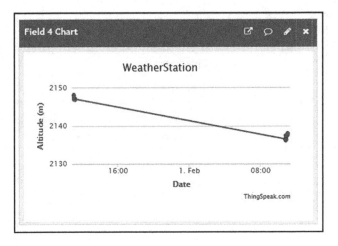

Figure 4-11. *Altitude graph*

Using Your Twitter Account in ThingSpeak

If you registered your Twitter account in Chapters 2 and 3, then it's not necessary to repeat this step. If this is not the case, you should click Apps ➤ ThingTweet. You must link your Twitter account. The system will provide you with an API Key.

Sending an Alert to Your Twitter Account

Click Apps and React. Then fill out the new React as follows (Figure 4-12):

React Name: WeatherStation – temperature

Condition type: Numeric

Test Frequency: On data insertion

Condition: If channel WeatherStation temperature is greater than 25

Action: ThingTweet

Then tweet: "From WeatherStation – temperature is above 25 degrees Celsius"

Using Twitter account: "YOUR TWITTER LOGIN"

Options: Run action only the first time the condition is met.

Figure 4-12. *Create a new React and fill in this data for the temperature*

Do the same with the humidity React data:

React Name: WeatherStation – humidity

Condition type: Numeric

Test Frequency: On data insertion

Condition: If channel WeatherStation humidity is greater than 45

Action: ThingTweet

Then tweet: "From WeatherStation – humidity is above 45 %"

Using Twitter account: "YOUR TWITTER LOGIN"

Options: Run action only the first time the condition is met.

Now you can get the next tweet alert (Figure 4-13).

Figure 4-13. *Alert sent to my Twitter account*

Challenges

Use the next sensors: DHT22, BMP180, and BMP280.

Conclusion

In this chapter, you used the 12C and One Wire protocols to build a weather station with your Raspberry Pi. Additionally, you tested the ThingSpeak server to display four graphs of your IoT system.

CHAPTER 5

Digital Image Processing with Python and OpenCV

OpenCV means Open Source Computer Vision Library. It is an open source computer vision library and it has bindings for C++, Python, and Java. It is used for a very wide range of applications including medical image analysis, stitching street view images, surveillance video, detecting and recognizing faces, tracking moving objects, extracting 3D models, and much more. OpenCV can take advantage of multicore processing and features GPU acceleration for real-time operation.

In this chapter, I will explain how to install OpenCV on your Raspberry Pi 3B. The main goal of this project is to make use of digital image processing with OpenCV and your Raspberry Pi 3B. To achieve this goal, you will start from the installation to make your own object classifiers and finally make an example where you can manipulate an object by means of an image in movement. This has many applications, ranging from recognizing people or objects to creating your own video surveillance system.

What will you do in this chapter?

- Software installation
- Creation of your object classifier
- Testing with images, videos, and a robot arm

© Guillermo Guillen 2019
G. Guillen, *Sensor Projects with Raspberry Pi*,
https://doi.org/10.1007/978-1-4842-5299-4_5

Installing the Software

In this section, you will install OpenCV. To do so, you must first type the
following commands to update your OS system. The results are shown in
Figures 5-1 and 5-2.

```
sudo apt-get update
```

and

```
sudo apt-get upgrade
```

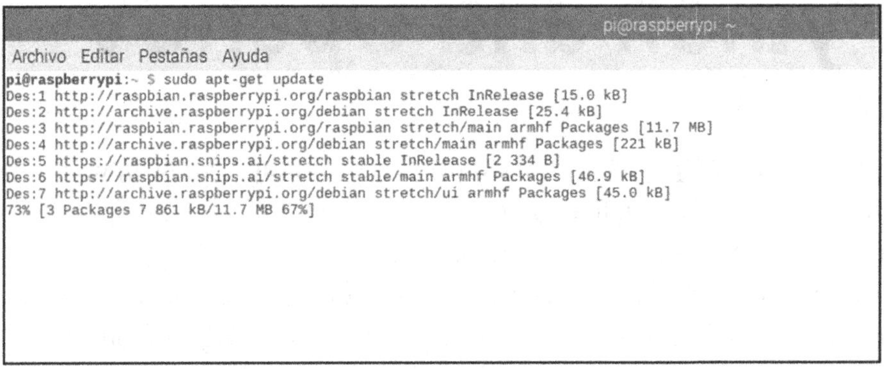

Figure 5-1. command: sudo apt-get update

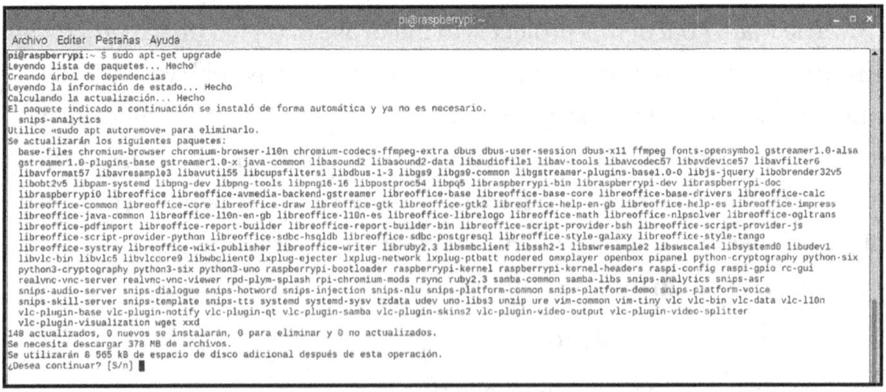

Figure 5-2. command: sudo apt-get upgrade

The following sections review the eight steps to correctly install Open CV on the Raspberry Pi 3B board.

Step 1: Installing Python 2.7 and 3

You must choose which version of Python you are going to work with. You need this code in order to enable Python in Open CV (Figure 5-3):

```
sudo apt-get install python2.7-dev
```

```
pi@raspberrypi:~ $ sudo apt-get install python2.7-dev
Leyendo lista de paquetes... Hecho
Creando árbol de dependencias
Leyendo la información de estado... Hecho
python2.7-dev ya está en su versión más reciente (2.7.13-2+deb9u3).
fijado python2.7-dev como instalado manualmente.
0 actualizados, 0 nuevos se instalarán, 0 para eliminar y 0 no actualizados.
pi@raspberrypi:~ $ ▮
```

Figure 5-3. *command: sudo apt-get install python2.7-dev*

For Python 3, type

```
sudo apt-get install python3-dev
```

Step 2: Installing Dependencies

Next, install the following useful libraries for OpenCV configuration (Figures 5-4 through 5-9). If any of these libraries don't get installed properly or the system fails, try again to avoid having errors.

```
sudo apt-get install build-essential cmake pkg-config
```

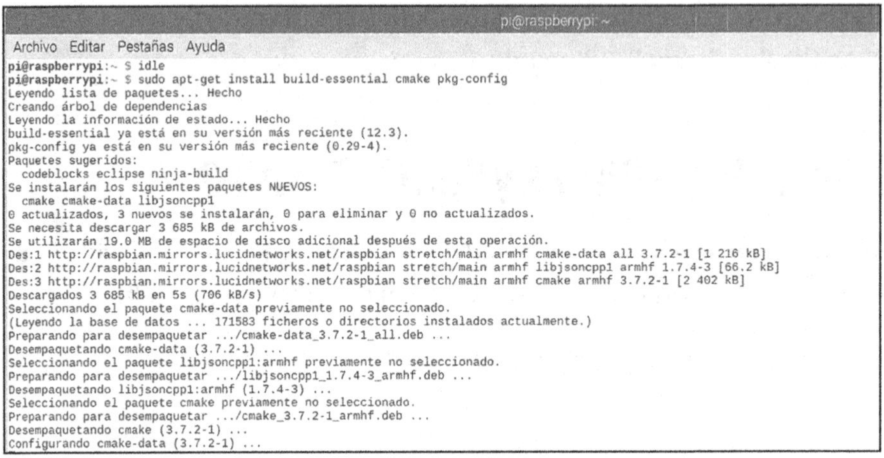

Figure 5-4. *command: sudo apt-get install build-essential cmake pkg-config*

```
sudo apt-get install libjpeg-dev libtiff5-dev libjasper-dev
libpng12-dev
```

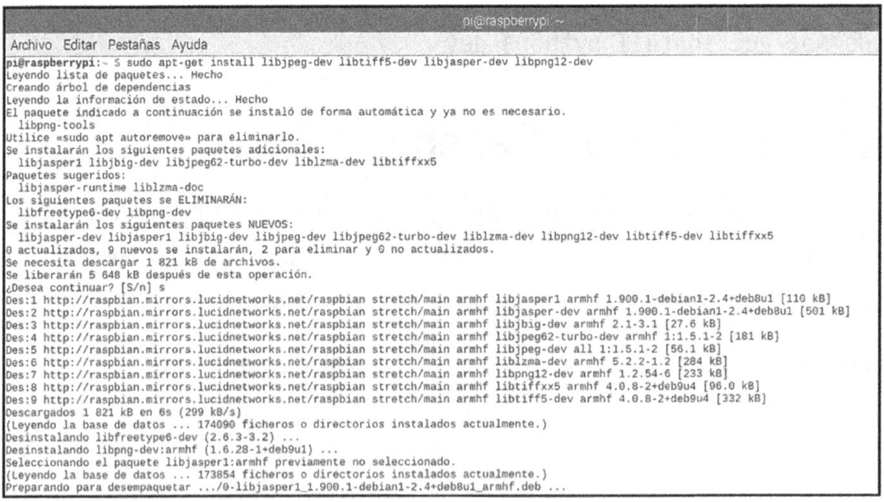

Figure 5-5. *command: sudo apt-get install libjpeg-dev libtiff5-dev libjasper-dev libpng12-dev*

```
sudo apt-get install libavcodec-dev libavformat-dev libswscale-
dev libv4l-dev
```

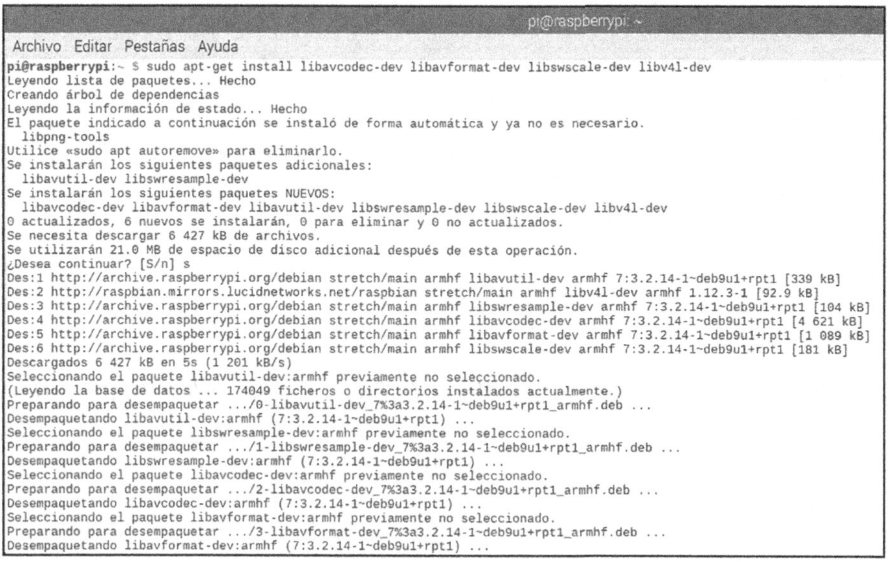

Figure 5-6. *command: sudo apt-get install libavcodec-dev libavformat-dev libswscale-dev libv4l-dev*

```
sudo apt-get install libxvidcore-dev libx264-dev
```

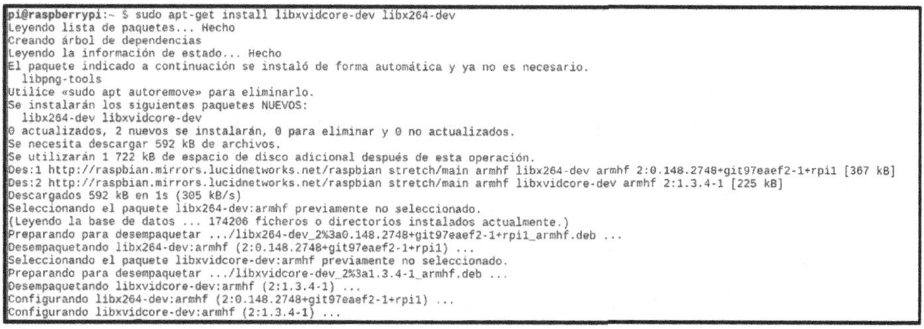

Figure 5-7. *command: sudo apt-get install libxvidcore-dev libx264-dev*

```
sudo apt-get install libgtk2.0-dev libgtk-3-dev
```

```
pi@raspberrypi:~ $ sudo apt-get install libgtk2.0-dev libgtk-3-dev
Leyendo lista de paquetes... Hecho
Creando árbol de dependencias
Leyendo la información de estado... Hecho
Se instalarán los siguientes paquetes adicionales:
  autoconf automake autopoint autotools-dev debhelper dh-autoreconf dh-strip-nondeterminism gettext gir1.2-atspi-2.0 gir1.2-gtk-2.0 icu-devtools
  intltool-debian libarchive-zip-perl libatk-bridge2.0-dev libatk1.0-dev libatspi2.0-dev libcairo-script-interpreter2 libcairo2-dev libdbus-1-dev
  libepoxy-dev libfile-stripnondeterminism-perl libfontconfig1-dev libfreetype6-dev libgdk-pixbuf2.0-dev libglib2.0-dev libgraphite2-dev libharfbuzz-dev
  libharfbuzz-gobject0 libice-dev libicu-dev libltdl-dev libmail-sendmail-perl libpango1.0-dev libpcre3-dev libpcre32-3 libpcrecpp0v5 libpixman-1-dev
  libpng-dev libpthread-stubs0-dev libsigsegv2 libsm-dev libsys-hostname-long-perl libtimedate-perl libtool libx11-dev libx11-doc libxau-dev
  libxcb-render0-dev libxcb-shm0-dev libxcb1-dev libxcomposite-dev libxcursor-dev libxdamage-dev libxdmcp-dev libxext-dev libxfixes-dev libxft-dev
  libxi-dev libxinerama-dev libxkbcommon-dev libxml2-utils libxrandr-dev libxrender-dev libxtst-dev m4 po-debconf x11proto-composite-dev x11proto-core-dev
  x11proto-damage-dev x11proto-fixes-dev x11proto-input-dev x11proto-kb-dev x11proto-randr-dev x11proto-record-dev x11proto-render-dev x11proto-xext-dev
  x11proto-xinerama-dev xorg-sgml-doctools xtrans-dev
Paquetes sugeridos:
  autoconf-archive gnu-standards autoconf-doc dh-make gettext-doc libasprintf-dev libgettextpo-dev libcairo2-doc libglib2.0-doc libgtk-3-doc libgtk2.0-doc
  libice-doc icu-doc libtool-doc imagemagick libpango1.0-doc libsm-doc gfortran | fortran95-compiler gcj-jdk libxcb-doc libxext-doc m4-doc
  libmail-box-perl
Los siguientes paquetes se ELIMINARÁN:
  libpng12-dev
Se instalarán los siguientes paquetes NUEVOS:
  autoconf automake autopoint autotools-dev debhelper dh-autoreconf dh-strip-nondeterminism gettext gir1.2-atspi-2.0 gir1.2-gtk-2.0 icu-devtools
  intltool-debian libarchive-zip-perl libatk-bridge2.0-dev libatk1.0-dev libatspi2.0-dev libcairo-script-interpreter2 libcairo2-dev libdbus-1-dev
  libepoxy-dev libfile-stripnondeterminism-perl libfontconfig1-dev libfreetype6-dev libgdk-pixbuf2.0-dev libglib2.0-dev libgraphite2-dev libgtk-3-dev
  libgtk2.0-dev libharfbuzz-dev libharfbuzz-gobject0 libice-dev libicu-dev libltdl-dev libmail-sendmail-perl libpango1.0-dev libpcre3-dev libpcre32-3
  libpcrecpp0v5 libpixman-1-dev libpng-dev libpthread-stubs0-dev libsigsegv2 libsm-dev libsys-hostname-long-perl libtimedate-perl libtool libx11-dev
  libx11-doc libxau-dev libxcb-render0-dev libxcb-shm0-dev libxcb1-dev libxcomposite-dev libxcursor-dev libxdamage-dev libxdmcp-dev libxext-dev
  libxfixes-dev libxft-dev libxi-dev libxinerama-dev libxkbcommon-dev libxml2-utils libxrandr-dev libxrender-dev libxtst-dev m4 po-debconf
  x11proto-composite-dev x11proto-core-dev x11proto-damage-dev x11proto-fixes-dev x11proto-input-dev x11proto-kb-dev x11proto-randr-dev
  x11proto-record-dev x11proto-render-dev x11proto-xext-dev x11proto-xinerama-dev xorg-sgml-doctools xtrans-dev
0 actualizados, 81 nuevos se instalarán, 1 para eliminar y 0 no actualizados.
Se necesita descargar 45.2 MB/45.4 MB de archivos.
Se utilizarán 174 MB de espacio de disco adicional después de esta operación.
¿Desea continuar? [S/n] s
```

***Figure 5-8.** command: sudo apt-get install libgtk2.0-dev libgtk-3-dev*

```
sudo apt-get install libatlas-base-dev gfortran
```

```
pi@raspberrypi:~ $ sudo apt-get install libatlas-base-dev gfortran
Leyendo lista de paquetes... Hecho
Creando árbol de dependencias
Leyendo la información de estado... Hecho
No se pudieron instalar algunos paquetes. Esto puede significar que
usted pidió una situación imposible o, si está usando la distribución
inestable, que algunos paquetes necesarios aún no se han creado o se
han sacado de «Incoming».
La siguiente información puede ayudar a resolver la situación:

Los siguientes paquetes tienen dependencias incumplidas:
 libatlas-base-dev : Depende: libatlas3-base (= 3.10.3-1+rpi1) pero 3.10.3-1-snips va a ser instalado
E: No se pudieron corregir los problemas, usted ha retenido paquetes rotos.
```

***Figure 5-9.** command: sudo apt-get install libatlas-base-dev gfortran*

Step 3: Getting the Latest OpenCV Source Code

I'm using version 3.3.0 of OpenCV. You can check the releases section of the official site to see the current build number. If your desired version is different, update the commands and paths below accordingly.

Download (Figure 5-10) and unzip OpenCV 3.3.0 (Figure 5-11) and its experimental modules (which are stored in the opencv_contrib repository):

```
wget -O opencv.zip
https://github.com/opencv/opencv/archive/3.3.0.zip
```

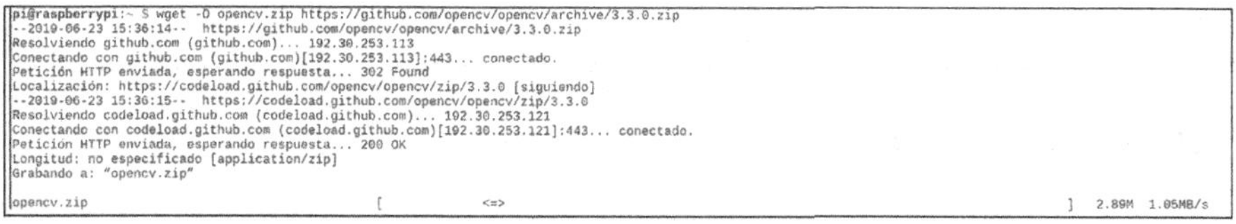

Figure 5-10. *Dowloading OpenCV*

```
wget -O opencv_contrib.zip
https://github.com/opencv/opencv_contrib/archive/3.3.0.zip
```

Figure 5-11. *Dowloading OpenCV contrib*

```
unzip opencv.zip
```

```
unzip opencv_contrib.zip
```

Step 4: Installing pip and virtualenv

These are the lowest-level tools for managing Python packages. Get pip first (Figure 5-12):

```
wget -O get-pip.py https://bootstrap.pypa.io/get-pip.py
sudo python get-pip.py
sudo python3 get-pip.py
```

Figure 5-12. *Getting the pip package*

Then, install the virtual environments (Figure 5-13):

```
sudo pip install virtualenv virtualenvwrapper
```

Figure 5-13. *Installing the pip package*

Modify your

```
sudo nano ~/.profile
```

Add the following lines (Figure 5-14):

```
export WORKONHOME=$HOME/.virtualenvs
export VIRTUALENVWRAPPER_PYTHON=/usr/bin/python2
source /usr/local/bin/virtualenvwrapper.sh
```

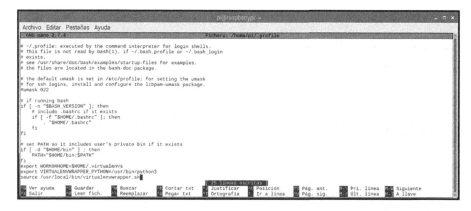

Figure 5-14. *Making changes to the profile file*

And activate the changes in Figure 5-15:

source ~/.profile

```
pi@raspberrypi:~ $ sudo nano ~/.profile
pi@raspberrypi:~ $ source ~/.profile
pi@raspberrypi:~ $
```

Figure 5-15. *Activating the changes*

Step 5: Creating a Virtual Environment

mkvirtualenv cv -p python2

Or, if you want to use Python 2.7 (this is what I am using in Figure 5-16) instead of Python 3:

mkvirtualenv cv -p python3

```
pi@raspberrypi:~ $ mkvirtualenv cv -p python2
Running virtualenv with interpreter /usr/bin/python2
Already using interpreter /usr/bin/python2
New python executable in /home/pi/.virtualenvs/cv/bin/python2
Not overwriting existing python script /home/pi/.virtualenvs/cv/bin/python (you must use /home/pi/.virtualenvs/cv/bin/python2)
Installing setuptools, pip, wheel...
done.
(cv) pi@raspberrypi:~ $
```

Figure 5-16. *Creating a virtual environment*

In your case, you can activate a virtualenv called cv:

```
pi@raspberrypi:~ $ workon cv
cv) pi@raspberrypi:~ $
```

Step 6: Installing Numpy and Scipy

Now that you are inside your virtual environment (as evidenced by the (cv) prefix in your terminal window), let's install some additional packages for data analysis: numpy and scipy (Figure 5-17).

```
sudo pip install numpy scipy
```

```
(cv) pi@raspberrypi:~ $ sudo pip install numpy scipy
DEPRECATION: Python 2.7 will reach the end of its life on January 1st, 2020. Please upgrade your Python as Python 2.7 won't be maintained after that date.
pip will drop support for Python 2.7.
Looking in indexes: https://pypi.org/simple, https://www.piwheels.org/simple
Requirement already satisfied: numpy in /usr/lib/python2.7/dist-packages (1.12.1)
Collecting scipy
  Downloading https://files.pythonhosted.org/packages/a4/32/48b7882953d6dbbeea9e4259a5d42258d6e77d1d6f80f9298d82af444af4/scipy-1.2.2.tar.gz (23.1MB)
                                          | 13.4MB 1.5MB/s eta 0:00:07
```

Figure 5-17. Installing numpy and scipy

Step 7: Installing OpenCV

Note   This will take a long, long, long time. This took almost three hours on my device. Also, your Raspberry Pi will overheat without proper cooling.

Again, I'm using version 3.3.0 of OpenCV. If you aren't, update your paths accordingly, as shown in Figure 5-18 and 5-19. Check that there are no errors (Figure 5-20).

```
cd ~/opencv-3.3.0/
mkdir build
cd build
```

```
(cv) pi@raspberrypi:~ $ cd ~/opencv-3.3.0/
(cv) pi@raspberrypi:~/opencv-3.3.0 $ mkdir build
(cv) pi@raspberrypi:~/opencv-3.3.0 $ cd build
(cv) pi@raspberrypi:~/opencv-3.3.0/build $ █
```

Figure 5-18. *Preparing the OpenCV installation*

```
cmake -D CMAKE_BUILD_TYPE=RELEASE \
    -D CMAKE_INSTALL_PREFIX=/usr/local \
    -D INSTALL_PYTHON_EXAMPLES=ON \
    -D OPENCV_EXTRA_MODULES_PATH=~/opencv_contrib-3.3.0/modules \
    -D BUILD_EXAMPLES=ON ..
```

```
(cv) pi@raspberrypi:~/opencv-3.3.0/build $ cmake -D CMAKE_BUILD_TYPE=RELEASE \
>     -D CMAKE_INSTALL_PREFIX=/usr/local \
>     -D INSTALL_PYTHON_EXAMPLES=ON \
>     -D OPENCV_EXTRA_MODULES_PATH=~/opencv_contrib-3.3.0/modules \
>     -D BUILD_EXAMPLES=ON ..
-- The CXX compiler identification is GNU 6.3.0
-- The C compiler identification is GNU 6.3.0
-- Check for working CXX compiler: /usr/bin/c++
-- Check for working CXX compiler: /usr/bin/c++ -- works
-- Detecting CXX compiler ABI info
-- Detecting CXX compiler ABI info - done
-- Detecting CXX compile features
█
```

Figure 5-19. *Using cmake*

```
                                          pi@raspberrypi: ~/opencv-3.3.0/build
Archivo  Editar  Pestañas  Ayuda
--     packages path:              lib/python3.5/site-packages
--
--   Python (for build):          /home/pi/.virtualenvs/cv/bin/python2.7
--
--   Java:
--     ant:                       /usr/bin/ant (ver 1.9.9)
--     JNI:                       NO
--     Java wrappers:             NO
--     Java tests:                NO
--
--   Matlab:                      Matlab not found or implicitly disabled
--
--   Documentation:
--     Doxygen:                   NO
--
--   Tests and samples:
--     Tests:                     YES
--     Performance tests:         YES
--     C/C++ Examples:            YES
--
--   Install path:                /usr/local
--
--   cvconfig.h is in:            /home/pi/opencv-3.3.0/build
-- ---------------------------------------------------------------
--
-- Configuring done
-- Generating done
-- Build files have been written to: /home/pi/opencv-3.3.0/build
(cv) pi@raspberrypi:~/opencv-3.3.0/build $ █
```

Figure 5-20. *There are no errors*

Now, get yourself a glass of beer and prepare for the final step:
compiling. To speed things up, temporarily increase the swap file size in
your PC, which is

```
sudo nano /etc/dphys-swapfile
```

by changing CONF_SWAPSIZE from 100 to 1024 (Figure 5-21):

```
# set size to absolute value, leaving empty (default) then uses
  computed value
#   you most likely don't want this, unless you have an special
    disk situation
#CONF_SWAPSIZE=100
CONF_SWAPSIZE=1024
```

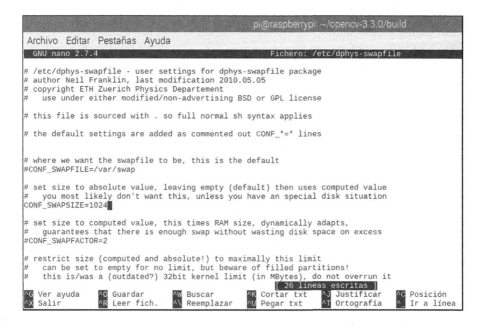

Figure 5-21. *Increasing the swap file size to 1024*

To avoid rebooting in order for these changes to take effect, simply restart the swap service (Figure 5-22):

```
sudo /etc/init.d/dphys-swapfile restart
```

Figure 5-22. *Restarting the swap service*

What I did (using all four CPU cores, as shown in Figure 5-23):

```
make -j4
```

```
(cv) pi@raspberrypi:~/opencv-3.3.0/build $ make -j4
Scanning dependencies of target carotene_objs
Scanning dependencies of target IlmImf
Scanning dependencies of target libwebp
Scanning dependencies of target libprotobuf
[  0%] Building CXX object 3rdparty/carotene/hal/carotene/CMakeFiles/carotene_objs.dir/src/absdiff.cpp.o
[  0%] Building C object 3rdparty/libwebp/CMakeFiles/libwebp.dir/dec/alpha_dec.c.o
[  0%] Building CXX object 3rdparty/openexr/CMakeFiles/IlmImf.dir/Half/half.cpp.o
[  0%] Building CXX object 3rdparty/protobuf/CMakeFiles/libprotobuf.dir/src/google/protobuf/arena.cc.o
[  0%] Building CXX object 3rdparty/carotene/hal/carotene/CMakeFiles/carotene_objs.dir/src/accumulate.cpp.o
[  0%] Building C object 3rdparty/libwebp/CMakeFiles/libwebp.dir/dec/buffer_dec.c.o
[  0%] Building C object 3rdparty/libwebp/CMakeFiles/libwebp.dir/dec/frame_dec.c.o
[  0%] Building CXX object 3rdparty/carotene/hal/carotene/CMakeFiles/carotene_objs.dir/src/add.cpp.o
[  0%] Building CXX object 3rdparty/carotene/hal/carotene/CMakeFiles/carotene_objs.dir/src/add_weighted.cpp.o
[  0%] Building CXX object 3rdparty/protobuf/CMakeFiles/libprotobuf.dir/src/google/protobuf/arenastring.cc.o
[  0%] Building C object 3rdparty/libwebp/CMakeFiles/libwebp.dir/dec/idec_dec.c.o
[  0%] Building CXX object 3rdparty/carotene/hal/carotene/CMakeFiles/carotene_objs.dir/src/bitwise.cpp.o
```

Figure 5-23. *With j4 you're using all four cores of your Raspberry Pi*

Once OpenCV compiles successfully, continue the installation:

```
sudo make install
sudo ldconfig
sudo apt-get update
```

Reboot the system and you should be good to go (Figure 5-24)!

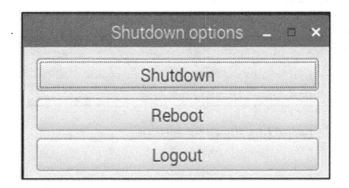

Figure 5-24. *Click the Reboot button*

Step 8: Testing the OpenCV Installation

Test the OpenCV installation as shown in Figure 5-25:

```
$ source ~/.profile
$ workon cv
$ python2
>>> import cv2
>>> cv2.__version__
'3.3.0'
>>>
```

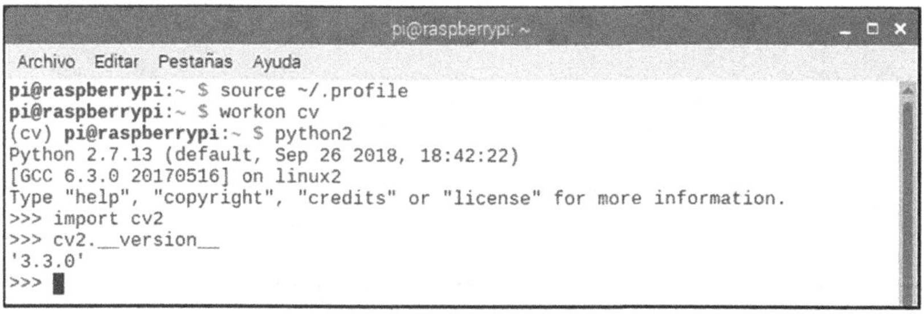

Figure 5-25. *My OpenCV version is 3.3.0*

If you are getting an error (Import Error: No module named 'cv2'), the library may be named incorrectly. You must search the cv2.so file (Figure 5-26).

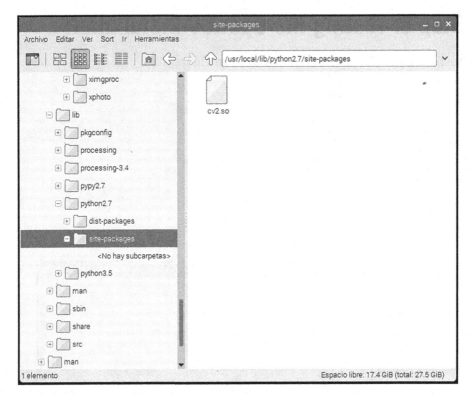

Figure 5-26. *Verifying the cv2.so file*

Fix it by renaming the library file to cv2.so:

```
cd /usr/local/lib/python3.5/site-packages/
```

```
sudo cp cv2.so /usr/local/lib/python2.7/site-packages/
```

If all goes well, you can uninstall the downloaded files since they only served to make the installation. I'm talking about opencv-3-3-0 and opencv_contrib-3.3.0.

In my case, I configured the versions of Python 2.7 and OpenCV 3.3.0, since they are compatible and also very stable. I suggest you work with stable versions.

After this detailed explanation of the Software installation, you can install this version of OpenCV, and try new versions that are recommended by advanced programmers. In the next section, you will develop your first object classifier, which will be used by OpenCV software.

Classifiers

You can make your own classifiers for recognition of people or objects. The following are the steps covered in the next sections to be successful in creating your classifier and using Windows:

1. Collect images for a database.

2. Arrange negative images.

3. Crop and mark positive images.

4. Create a vector of positive images.

5. Complete Haar training.

6. Create the XML file.

Step 1: Collecting Images for a Database

I recommend you collect 200 positive images and 200 negative images at least. Many classifiers use 500 or 1,000 images. I suggest you check out http://image-net.org/.

The positive images are those images that contain an object (e.g. face or eyes), and negatives are images that do not contain an object (Figure 5-27). Having the same number of positive and negative (background as shown in Figure 5-28) images will normally cause a more accurate classifier.

Figure 5-27. *Negative images*

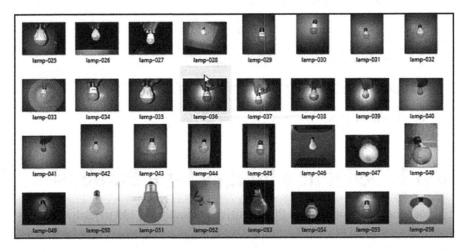

Figure 5-28. *Positive images*

Step 2: Arranging the Negative Images

Put your background images in folder ...\training\negative and run the batch file:

```
create_list.bat
dir /b *.jpg >bg.txt
```

After running this batch file, you will get a text file. Each line looks like the following:

image1200.jpg
image1201.jpg
image1202.jpg

...

Later, you will need this negative data file for training the classifier (Figure 5-29).

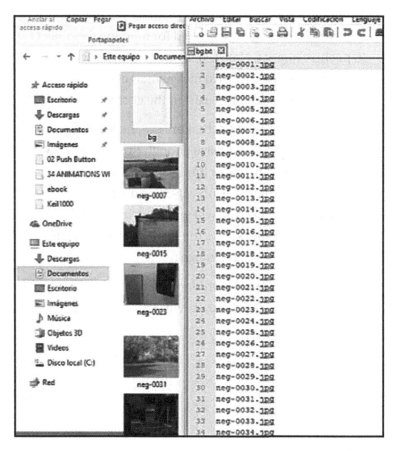

Figure 5-29. *Open the bg.txt file and verify the data*

Step 3: Cropping and Marking Positive Images

In this step, you need to create a data file (vector file) that contains the names of the positive images as well as the location of the objects in each image. You can create this file via *Objectmaker*. I will continue with *Objectmaker*, which is straightforward.

- In folder ..\training\positive\rawdata, put you positive images.

- In folder ..\training\positive, there is a file named objectmaker.exe that you need for marking the objects in positive images. Note that in order to correctly run objectmaker.exe, two files named cv.dll and highgui.dll should also exist in the current directory.

  - Before running objectmaker.exe, make sure you are relaxed and you have enough time to carefully mark and crop tens or hundreds of images! How should you mark the objects? Running the file objectmaker.exe you will see two windows like in Figure 5-30: one shows the loaded image, and the other one shows the image name.

  - Click at the top left corner of the object area, and hold the mouse left key down (Figure 5-30).

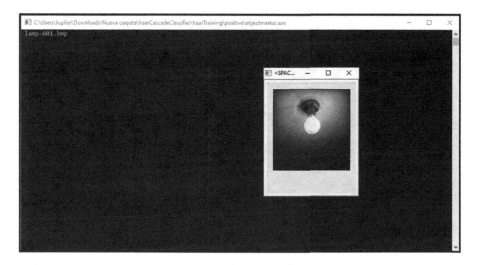

Figure 5-30. *The first image automatically opens*

- While keeping the left key down, drag the mouse to the bottom right corner of the object (Figure 5-31).

- You could be able to see a rectangle that surrounds the object. If you are not happy with your selection, press any key (except the spacebar and Enter) to undo your selection, and try to draw another rectangle again.

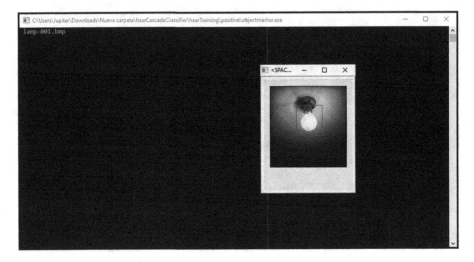

Figure 5-31. *Make a rectangle that surrounds the object*

- Important note: Take care to always start the bounding box at either the top left or bottom right corner. If you use the other two corners, objectmaker.exe will not write the coordinates of the selected object into the info.txt file.

- If you are happy with the selected rectangle, press the space bar. After that, the rectangle position and its size will appear in the left window (Figure 5-32).

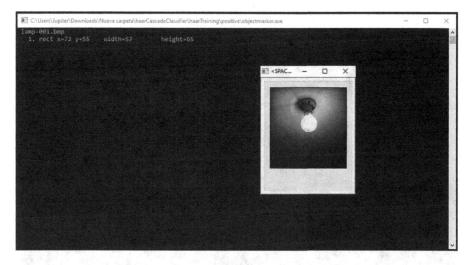

Figure 5-32. *Press the space bar and verify the data*

- Repeat these steps if there are multiple objects in the current image.

- When you finished with the current image, press the Enter key to load the next image (Figure 5-33.)

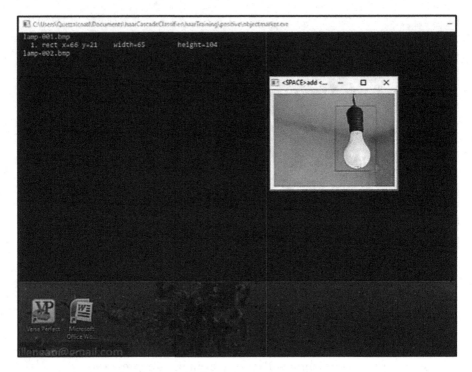

Figure 5-33. *Continue with the next image*

- Repeat the steps until all of the positive images load one by one, and finish.

If you feel tired and you want to stop it at the middle marking process, press the escape key.

- A file named info.txt will be created.

- When you escape Objectmaker and you want to continue later, create a backup for `info.txt` because every time you run `objectmarker.exe`, it overwrites the previous `info.txt` file without any notice. Since it creates an empty new `info.txt`, you will lose you

previous work! Make a backup numbered file (e.g.
info1.txt, info2.txt) any time you escape, and later
merge all your backups into a final info.txt.

- Within info.txt there will be some information like
  the following:

```
rawdata\image1200.bmp 1 34 12 74 24
rawdata\image1201.bmp 3 35 25 70 39 40 95 80 92 120 40 45 36
rawdata\image1202.bmp 2 10 24 90 90 45 68 99 82
```

The first number in each line defines the number of existing objects
in the given image. For example, in second line, the number **3** means that
you selected three objects within image1201.bmp. The next four numbers
(shown in green) define the location of first object in the image (top left
vertex: x=35, y=24, width=70, and height=39).

The next step is packing the object images into a vector file.

Step 4: Creating a Vector of Positive Images

In folder ..\training\ there is a batch file named samples_creation.bat.
The contents of the bath file (Figure 5-34) are as follows:

```
createsamples.exe -info positive/info.txt -vec vector/
facevector.vec -num
200 -w 24 -h 24
```

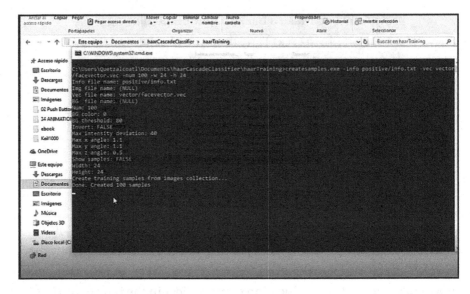

Figure 5-34. *Example of how to create a vector*

Main parameters:

- `info positive/info.txt` is the path for the positive info file

- `vec vector/facevector.vec` is the path for the output vector file

- num 200 is the number of positive files to be packed in a *vector file*

- w 24 is the width of the objects

- h 24 is the height of the objects

The batch file loads `info.txt` and packs the object images into a vector file, for example `facevector.vec`.

After running the batch file, you will have the file `facevector.vec` in the folder `..\training\vector`.

Note To run `creatsample.exe` you also need the files `cv097.dll`, `cxcore097.dll`, `highgui097.dll`, and `libguide40.dll` in the folder `..\training`.

Step 5: Haar Training

In folder `..\training`, you can modify the `haartraining.bat` (Figure 5-35):

```
haartraining.exe -data cascades -vec vector/vector.vec -bg
negative/bg.txt
```

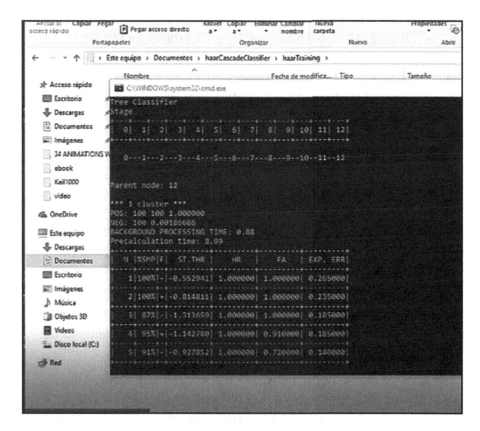

Figure 5-35. *Haar training example*

- npos 200 -nneg 200 -nstages 15 -mem 1024 -mode ALL -w 24 -h 24 –nonsym

- `data cascades` is the path for storing the cascade of classifiers

- `vec data/vector.vec` is the path of the vector file

- `bg negative/bg.txt` points to the background file

- npos 200 is the number of positive samples ≤ no. positive bmp files

- nneg 200 is the number of negative samples (patches) ≥ npos

- nstages 15 is the number of intended stages for training

- mem 1024 is the quantity of memory assigned in MB

- mode ALL (look in the literature for more info about this parameter)

- w 24 -h 24 is the sample size

- nonsym (use this if your subject is not horizontally symmetrical)

The size of –W and –H in `harrtraining.bat` should be same as what you defined in `sample-creation.bat`.

`Harrtraining.exe` collects a new set of negative samples for each stage, and –nneg sets the limit for the size of the set. It uses the previous stages' information to determine which of the "candidate samples" are misclassified. Training ends when the ratio of misclassified samples to candidate samples is lower.

Regardless of the number of stages (nstages) that you define in `haartraining.bat`, the program may terminate early if you reach the above condition. Although this is normally a good sign of accuracy in the training process, this also may happen when the number of positive images is not enough (e.g. less than 500).

Note   To run haartaining.exe you also need the files cv097. dll, cxcore097.dll, and highgui097.dll in the folder ..\ training.

Data provided in Figure 5-35 is related to the first stage of training:

- Parent node: Defines the current stage under the training process

- N: The number of used features in this stage

- %SMP: The sample percentage (percentage of sample used for this feature)

- F: "+" if flipped (when symmetry applied) and "–" if not

- ST.THR: Stage threshold

- HR: Hit rate based on the stage threshold

- FA: False alarm based on the stage threshold

- EXP. ERR: Exponential error of strong classifier

Step 6: Creating the XML File

After finishing the Haar training step, in folder ../training/cascades/ you should have catalogues named from 0 up to N-1, in which N is the number of stages you already defined in haartraining.bat.

In each of those catalogues there should be an AdaBoostCARTHaarClassifier.txt file. Copy all the folders 0..N-1 into the folder ../cascade2xml/data/.

Now you should combine all of the created stages (classifiers) into a single XML file which will be your final file of a "cascade of Haar-like classifiers."

Run the batch file `convert.bat` at `../cascade2xml/` which is

```
haarconv.exe data myfacedetector.xml 24 24
```

`myfacedetecor.xml` is the output file name and 24 24 are *W* and *H,* respectively.

Now you have your own XML file (Figure 5-36). Copy it into the `MyCascade` folder, point to this classifier from your project source code, and run your detection program.

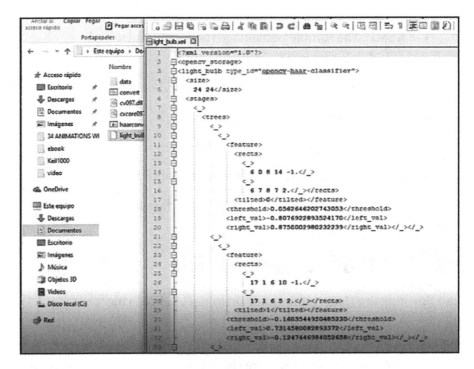

Figure 5-36. *Verifying the XML file*

Note   You can download the source code from the "Software" section at the end of this chapter.

Now that you already know how to make object classifiers, the next step is to apply them to detect objects in images and videos and to get a robot arm moving with a moving object.

Testing with Images

Here's the code to make a test with images already captured (as shown in Figure 5-37):

HaarcascadeBanana.py

```
********************

import numpy as np
import cv2

banana_cascade = cv2.CascadeClassifier('banana_classifier.xml')

img = cv2.imread('banana1.jpg')
gray = cv2.cvtColor(img, cv2.COLOR_BGR2GRAY)

bananas = banana_cascade.detectMultiScale(gray, 1.3, 5)
for (x,y,w,h) in bananas:
    img = cv2.rectangle(img,(x,y),(x+w,y+h),(255,0,0),2)

cv2.imshow('img',img)
cv2.waitKey(0)
cv2.destroyAllWindows()

********************
```

Figure 5-37. *Example of a test with an image*

Testing with Videos

Here is the code to do an object recognition test with a classifier and a webcam in a video (as shown in Figure 5-38):

HaarcascadeBananasVideo.py

```
********************

import numpy as np
import cv2

banana_cascade = cv2.CascadeClassifier('banana_classifier.xml')
cap = cv2.VideoCapture(0)

while 1:
    ret, img = cap.read()
    gray = cv2.cvtColor(img, cv2.COLOR_BGR2GRAY)
```

```
banana = banana_cascade.detectMultiScale(gray, 1.3, 5)
for (x,y,w,h) in banana:          cv2.rectangle(img,(x,y),
                                  (x+w,y+h),(255,0,0),2)
cv2.imshow('img',img)
k = cv2.waitKey(30) & 0xff
if k == 27:
    break
cap.release()
cv2.destroyAllWindows()
```

****

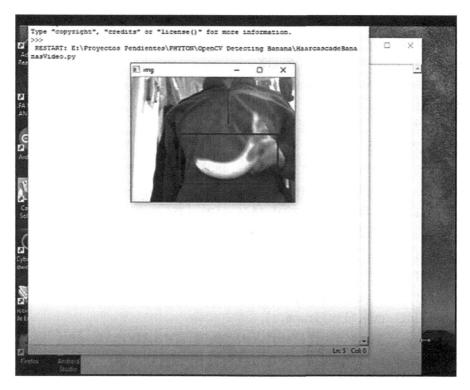

Figure 5-38.   *Example of a test with a video*

The following example recognizes faces and uses a webcam:
face_webcam.py

```
************************

import cv2
import numpy as np
import struct
import time
a=0
b=0
x=0
y=0
time.sleep(2)
font=cv2.FONT_HERSHEY_SIMPLEX
FaceCascade=cv2.CascadeClassifier('haarcascade_frontalface_
default.xml')
cap=cv2.VideoCapture(0)
def BoxDraw():
    cv2.line(flipit,(213,0),(213,480),(255,0,0),2)
    cv2.line(flipit,(426,0),(426,480),(255,0,0),2)
    cv2.line(flipit,(0,160),(640,160),(255,0,0),2)
    cv2.line(flipit,(0,320),(640,320),(255,0,0),2)
    pass
while True:
    ret,frame=cap.read()
    flipit=cv2.flip(frame,1)
    gray=cv2.cvtColor(flipit,cv2.COLOR_BGR2GRAY)
    face=FaceCascade.detectMultiScale(gray,1.2,4)

    try:
        for (x1,y1,w1,h1) in face:
            cv2.rectangle(flipit,(x1,y1),(x1+w1,y1+h1),(0,255,0),2)
```

```
    except:
        pass

    cv2.imshow('flipit',flipit)
    k=cv2.waitKey(20) & 0xff
    if k==27:
        break
cap.release()
cv2.destroyAllWindows()
```

****

This example also recognizes faces, but uses the camera of the Raspberry Pi:

face_picamera.py

****

```
# import the necessary packages
from picamera.array import PiRGBArray
from picamera import PiCamera
import time
import cv2

# initialize the camera and grab a reference to the raw camera
capture
camera = PiCamera()
camera.resolution = (640, 480)
camera.framerate = 32
rawCapture = PiRGBArray(camera, size=(640, 480))

#Load a cascade file for detecting faces
face_detector = cv2.CascadeClassifier('haarcascade_frontalface_
default.xml')
```

```
# allow the camera to warmup
time.sleep(0.1)
count = 0

# capture frames from the camera
for frame in camera.capture_continuous(rawCapture,
format="bgr", use_video_port=True):
        image = frame.array
        gray = cv2.cvtColor(image, cv2.COLOR_BGR2GRAY)
        faces = face_detector.detectMultiScale(gray, 1.3, 5)
        for (x,y,w,h) in faces:
                cv2.rectangle(image, (x,y), (x+w,y+h), (255,0,0), 2)
                count += 1
        # show the frame
        cv2.imshow("Frame", image)
        key = cv2.waitKey(1) & 0xFF

        # clear the stream in preparation for the next frame
        rawCapture.truncate(0)

        # if the `q` key was pressed, break from the loop
        if key == ord("q"):
                break
```

****

Moving a Robot Arm

Next is an example of how you can use your Raspberry Pi 3B to move a
robot arm when you are moving an object in front of your Raspberry Pi
camera or in front of a webcam. The camera of the Raspberry Pi detects
the object of your classifier and processes the data of its coordinates.

Immediately afterwards it sends the data through the serial port where your Arduino UNO board is connected (Figure 5-39). The servos move according to the angle X or Y as the case may be.

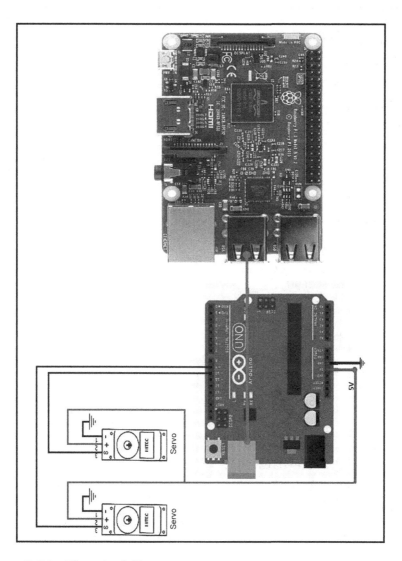

Figure 5-39. *Electrical diagram*

Here's the code used to move a robot arm and make use of an image. The code with Arduino is the following:

Robot_Arm.ino

```
********************
#include <Servo.h>
int data_x = 0;
int data_y = 0;
int data[1];
Servo myservo_x;
Servo myservo_y;

void setup() {
  Serial.begin(9600);
  myservo_x.attach(9);
  myservo_y.attach(10);
  myservo_x.write(90);
  myservo_y.write(90);
}

void loop() {
  while (Serial.available() >= 2) {
    for (int i = 0; i < 2; i++) {
      data[i] = Serial.read();
    }
    myservo_x.write(data[0]);
    myservo_y.write(data[1]);
    Serial.println(data[0]);
    Serial.println(data[1]);
  }
}

********************
```

The Python code with a webcam is the following:

Robot_Arm_Webcam.py

****

```python
import cv2
import numpy as np
import serial
import struct
import time
a=0
b=0
x=0
y=0
ser = serial.Serial('/dev/ttyACM0',9600)

time.sleep(2)
font=cv2.FONT_HERSHEY_SIMPLEX
FaceCascade=cv2.CascadeClassifier('haarcascade_frontalface_
default.xml')
cap=cv2.VideoCapture(0)
def BoxDraw():
    cv2.line(flipit,(213,0),(213,480),(255,0,0),2)
    cv2.line(flipit,(426,0),(426,480),(255,0,0),2)
    cv2.line(flipit,(0,160),(640,160),(255,0,0),2)
    cv2.line(flipit,(0,320),(640,320),(255,0,0),2)
    pass
while True:
    ret,frame=cap.read()
    flipit=cv2.flip(frame,1)
    gray=cv2.cvtColor(flipit,cv2.COLOR_BGR2GRAY)
    face=FaceCascade.detectMultiScale(gray,1.2,4)
    try:
```

```python
        for (x1,y1,w1,h1) in face:
            a=int((2*x1+w1)/2)
            b=int((2*y1+h1)/2)
            x=int(a/3.66)
            y=int(b/2.55)
            ser.write(struct.pack('>BB', x,y))
            cv2.rectangle(flipit,(x1,y1),(x1+w1,y1+h1),
            (0,255,0),2)

    except:
        pass

    cv2.imshow('flipit',flipit)
    k=cv2.waitKey(20) & 0xff
    if k==27:
        break
cap.release()
cv2.destroyAllWindows()
```

****

The Python code with the camera of the Raspberry Pi is the following and the test is shown in Figure 5-40:

****

```python
# import the necessary packages
from picamera.array import PiRGBArray
from picamera import PiCamera
import time
import cv2
import serial
import struct
a=0
```

```
b=0
x1=0
y1=0
ser = serial.Serial('/dev/ttyACM0',9600)

# initialize the camera and grab a reference to the raw camera
capture
camera = PiCamera()
camera.resolution = (640, 480)
camera.framerate = 32
rawCapture = PiRGBArray(camera, size=(640, 480))

#Load a cascade file for detecting faces
face_detector = cv2.CascadeClassifier('haarcascade_frontalface_
default.xml')

# allow the camera to warmup
time.sleep(0.1)
count = 0

# capture frames from the camera
for frame in camera.capture_continuous(rawCapture,
format="bgr", use_video_port=True):
        image = frame.array
        gray = cv2.cvtColor(image, cv2.COLOR_BGR2GRAY)
        faces = face_detector.detectMultiScale(gray, 1.3, 5)
        for (x,y,w,h) in faces:
                a=int((2*x+w)/2)
                b=int((2*y+h)/2)
                x1=int(a/3.66)
                y1=int(b/2.55)
                ser.write(struct.pack('>BB', x1,y1))
                cv2.rectangle(image, (x,y), (x+w,y+h), (255,0,0), 2)
```

```
            count += 1
# show the frame
cv2.imshow("Frame", image)
key = cv2.waitKey(1) & 0xFF

# clear the stream in preparation for the next frame
rawCapture.truncate(0)

# if the `q` key was pressed, break from the loop
if key == ord("q"):
        break
```

****

Figure 5-40. *Test with a robot arm*

Software

The complete source code and libraries can be found at `https://drive.google.com/file/d/1bTCalgFRTBjExgXsRFN85ehEl5ujafhH/view?usp=sharing`.

Here you can get the next source code sections:

- Chapter_5_3

- Chapter_5_4

- Chapter_5_5

- Chapter_5_6

Challenges

1. Develop a spoon detection system using the Haar Cascade classifier.

2. Develop a system that detects spoons or spotlights, and indicate where these objects are located.

Conclusion

In this chapter, you made an application for digital image processing and you used a Haar Cascade classifier. You verified the application with the Raspberry Pi camera and a webcam.

This is the conclusion of this book. You learned basic and advanced concepts of the Python programming language, which is widely used with Raspberry Pi boards. You explored the world of the Internet of Things, which has had a boom in recent years, and its scope is incalculable in any field of technology. Another important issue you explored is digital image processing, which is currently being used in artificial intelligence. If you had no problems with the projects in this book, congratulations. There are more complex things waiting for you! But if you feel that all of this is very difficult, it's ok; I want to tell you that it was not easy for me to get this information and confirm it.

Much of this information is being updated daily and I advise you to update your projects. How? For example, you can participate in contests by companies that sell hardware. They offer new products and invite everyone to make innovations. You can also check the official information from government agencies that generate science such as NASA, ESA, or prestigious universities. I will surely update or expand this information in the future.

APPENDIX

Hardware Specifications

It's important to know the technical specifications of the hardware used in this book in order to understand the designs. You may also need to know the pins on the hardware to make the correct connections and to avoid short circuits that could damage your development boards.

© Guillermo Guillen 2019
G. Guillen, *Sensor Projects with Raspberry Pi*,
https://doi.org/10.1007/978-1-4842-5299-4

Raspberry Pi 3B

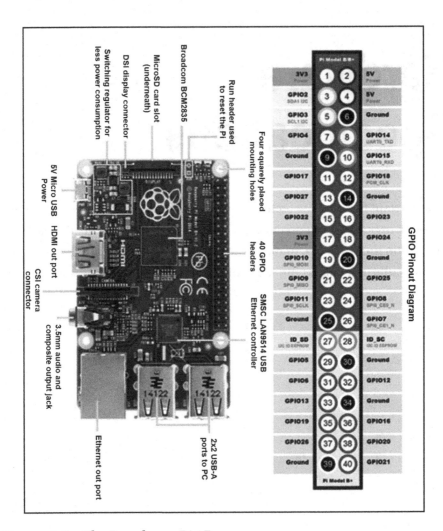

Figure A-1. *The Raspberry Pi 3B*

The Raspberry Pi 3B board is shown in Figure A-1.

Technical Specifications

Processor

- Broadcom BCM2387 chipset

- 1.2GHz quad-core ARM Cortex-A53 (64-bit)

- 802.11 b/g/n Wireless LAN and Bluetooth 4.1 (Bluetooth Classic and LE)

- IEEE 802.11 b/g/n Wi-Fi. Protocol: WEP, WPA WPA2, algorithms AES-CCMP (maximum keylength of 256 bits), maximum range of 100 meters

- IEEE 802.15 Bluetooth, symmetric encryption algorithm Advanced Encryption Standard (AES) with 128-bit key, maximum range of 50 meters

GPU

- Dual-core VideoCore IV® multimedia co-processor with Open GL ES 2.0, hardware-accelerated Open VG, and 1080p30 H.264 high-profile decode

- Capable of 1Gpixel/s, 1.5Gtexel/s, or 24GFLOPs with texture filtering and DMA infrastructure

Memory

- 1GB LPDDR2

Operating System

- Boots from Micro SD card, running a version of the Linux operating system or Windows 10 IoT

Dimensions

- 85 x 56 x 17mm

Power

- Micro USB socket 5V1, 2.5A

Connectors

Ethernet

- 10/100 BaseT Ethernet socket

Video Output

- HDMI (rev 1.3 and 1.4)

- Composite RCA (PAL and NTSC)

Audio Output

- Audio output 3.5mm jack

- HDMI

- USB 4 x USB 2.0 connector

GPIO Connector

- 40-pin 2.54 mm (100 mil) expansion header: 2 x 20 strip

- Provides 27 GPIO pins as well as +3.3V, +5V, and GND supply lines

Camera Connector

- 15-pin MIPI Camera Serial Interface (CSI-2)

Display Connector

- Display Serial Interface (DSI) 15-way flat flex cable connector with two data lanes and a clock lane

Memory Card Slot

- Push/pull Micro SDIO

Raspberry Pi Zero W

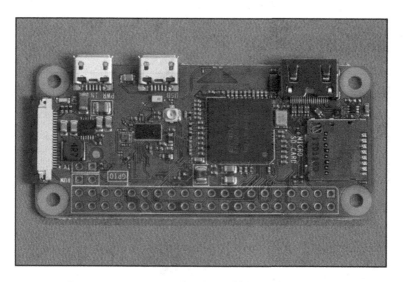

Figure A-2. *The Raspberry Pi Zero W*

The Raspberry Pi Zero W (Figure A-2) was launched at the end of February 2017. The Pi Zero W has all the functionality of the original Pi Zero but with added connectivity, consisting of

- 802.11 b/g/n Wireless LAN

- Bluetooth 4.1

- Bluetooth Low Energy

Like the Pi Zero, it also has

- 1GHz, single-core CPU

- 512MB RAM

- Mini HDMI and USB On-The-Go ports

- Micro USB power

- HAT-compatible 40-pin header

- Composite video and reset headers

- CSI camera connector

PIR Motion Sensor

Figure A-3. *The PIR motion sensor*

The PIR motion sensor (Figure A-3) is a highly integrated module popularly used for entry detection. It is compatible with a microcontroller or DC loads.

Advantages

- Simple, easy-to-adopt system

- There are two adjustable potentiometers on the module. You can use them to change the trigger sensitivity and the duration of the trigger signal.

Specifications

- Input voltage: DC 4.5-20V

- Static current: 50uA

- Output signal: 0,3V, or 5V (output high when motion detected)

- Sentry angle: 110 degrees

- Sentry distance: Max 7m

- Shunt for setting override trigger: H - Yes, L – No

- Module type: Sensor

- Weight: 15.00g

- Board size: NULL

- Version: 1.0

- Operation level: Digital 5V

- Power supply external: 5V

MQ2 Gas Sensor

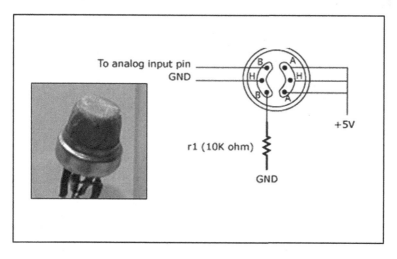

Figure A-4. *MQ2 gas sensor*

The sensitive material of the MQ2 gas sensor (Figure A-4) is SnO2, which with lower conductivity in clean air. When the target combustible gas exists, the sensor's conductivity is higher along with the gas concentration rising. Please use a simple electro circuit. Convert the change of conductivity to correspond to the output signal of the gas concentration.

The MQ2 gas sensor has a high sensitivity to LPG, propane, and hydrogen; it can also be used with methane and other combustible steam. It is a low-cost sensor and is suitable for different applications.

Characteristics

- Good sensitivity to combustible gas in a wide range

- High sensitivity to LPG, propane, and hydrogen

- Long life and low cost

- Simple drive circuit

Applications

- Domestic gas leakage detector

- Industrial combustible gas detector

- Portable gas detector

ADS1115

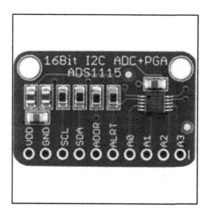

Figure A-5. *The ADS1115*

The ADS1115 is shown in Figure A-5.

Features

- Ultra-small QFN package: 2mm x 1.5mm x 0.4mm

- Wide supply range: 2.0V to 5.5v

- Low current consumption:

  Continuous mode: Only 150 Ua

  Single-shoot mode: Auto shut-down

- Programmable data rate: 8SPS to 860SPS

- Internal low-drift

- Voltage reference

- Internal oscillator

- Internal PGA

- 12C interface: Pin-selectable addresses

- Four single-ended or two differential inputs (ADS1115)

- Programmable comparator (ADS1114 and DS1115)

Applications

- Portable instrumentation

- Consumer goods

- Battery monitoring

- Temperature measurement

- Factory automation and process controls

BMP085 Pressure Sensor

Figure A-6. *The BMP085 pressure sensor*

The BMP085 pressure sensor is shown in Figure A-6.

Description

This precision sensor from Bosch is the best low-cost sensing solution for measuring barometric pressure and temperature. Because pressure changes with altitude, you can also use it as an altimeter. The sensor is soldered onto a PCB with a 3.3V regulator, I2C level shifter, and pull-up resistors on the I2C pins.

There's also a fully 5V compliant version of this board. A 3.3V regulator and an I2c level shifter circuit are included so you can use this sensor safely with 5V logic and power.

Using the sensor is easy. For example, if you're using an Arduino, simply connect the VIN pin to the 5V voltage pin, GND to ground, SCL to I2C Clock (Analog 5), and SDA to I2C Data (Analog 4). Then download the BMP085 Arduino library and example code for temperature, pressure, and altitude calculation. Install the library, and load the example sketch. Immediately you'll have precision temperature, pressure, and altitude data. We also have a detailed tutorial so you can understand the sensor in depth, including how to properly calculate altitude based on sea-level barometric pressure.

Technical Details

- Vin: 3 to 5 VDC

- Logic: 3 to 5V compliant

- I2C 7-bit address 0x77

- Pressure sensing range: 300-1100 hPa (9000m to -500m above sea level)

- Up to 0.03hPa/0.25m resolution

- -40 to +85°C operational range, +-2°C temperature accuracy

DHT11 Humidity Sensor

Figure A-7. *The DHT11 Humidity sensor*

The DHT11 humidity sensor is shown in Figure A-7.

Features and Applications

- Full range temperature compensated
- Relative humidity and temperature measurement
- Calibrated digital signal
- Outstanding long-term stability
- Extra components not needed
- Long transmission distance
- Low power consumption
- 4-pin package and fully interchangeable

Description

The sensor offers a DHT11 output calibrated digital signal. It utilizes
an exclusive digital-signal-collecting technique and humidity sensing
technology, assuring its reliability and stability. Its sensing elements are
connected with an 8-bit single-chip computer.

Every sensor of this model is temperature compensated and calibrated
in accurate calibration chamber and the calibration coefficient is saved in
OTP memory.

It has a small size, low power consumption, and long transmission
distance (20m), enabling the DHT11 to be suited to all kinds of harsh
application occasions. The single-row package with four pins makes the
connection very convenient.

Technical Specifications

- Power supply: 3-5.5V DC

- Output signal digital signal via single bus

- Sensing element: Polymer resistor

- Measuring range: Humidity 20-90%RH; temperature
  0-50 Celsius

- Accuracy humidity: Humidity +-4%RH (max +-5%RH);
  temperature +-2.0 Celsius

- Resolution or sensitivity: Humidity 1%RH; temperature
  0.1 Celsius

- Repeatability: Humidity +-1%RH; temperature
  +-1 Celsius

- Humidity hysteresis: +-1%RH

- Long-term stability: +-0.5%RH/year

- Sensing period average: 2s

- Interchangeability: Fully interchangeable

- Dimensions: 12 x 15.5 x 5.5mm

Index

© Guillermo Guillen 2019
G. Guillen, *Sensor Projects with Raspberry Pi*,
https://doi.org/10.1007/978-1-4842-5299-4

Printed in the United States
By Bookmasters